Ctrl+N	Creates a new workbook
Ctrl+O	Opens an existing workbook
Ctrl+S	Saves the active workbook
Ctrl+P	Prints the active workbook
Ctrl+B	Emboldens (or removes emboldening)
Ctrl+I	Italicises (or removes italicisation)
Ctrl+U	Underlines (or removes underlining)
Ctrl+F	Launches a find operation
Ctrl+H	Launches a find-and-replace operation
Ctrl+A	Selects all cells in the active worksheet
Ctrl+Z	Undoes the previous editing operation
Ctrl+Y	Reverses Undo
Ctrl+G	Launches the Go To dialog
Ctrl+Page Down	Moves to the next worksheet
Ctrl+Page Up	Moves to the previous worksheet
Ctrl+Home	Moves to the start of the active worksheet
Ctrl+1	Launches the Format Cells dialog
Ctrl+`	Toggle between displaying and hiding formulas
Ctrl+;	Inserts the current date
Ctrl+Shift+;	Inserts the current time
Shift+Spacebar	Selects the current row
Ctrl+Spacebar	Selects the current column
F1	Launches the Office Assist
F2	Launches Edit Mode
Shift+F3	Launches the Paste Funct
F7	Launches a spell check
F8	Toggles Selection mode
Alt+F8	Launches the Macro dia
F9	Performs a manual cal

About the Series

In easy steps series is developed for time-sensitive people who want results fast. It is designed for quick, easy and effortless learning.

By using the best authors in the field, combined with our in-house expertise in computing, this series is ideal for all computer users. It explains the essentials clearly and concisely – without the unnecessary verbal blurb. We strive to ensure that each book is technically superior, effective for easy learning and offers the best value.

Learn the essentials **in easy steps** – accept no substitutes! Titles in the series include:

General	Microsoft Works	Sage Instant Accounting
Design and Typography	PowerPoint	Sage Line 50
Networking	SmartSuite	Sage Sterling for Windows
PCs	Word 97	**Internet**
Shareware	Word	AOL UK
Upgrading Your PC	WordPerfect	CompuServe UK
Year 2000	**Graphics and DTP**	FrontPage
Operating Systems	AutoCAD	HTML
Psion 5	AutoCAD LT	Internet Culture
Windows 98	CorelDRAW	Internet Directory UK
Windows 95	Illustrator	Internet Explorer 4
Windows CE	PageMaker	Internet UK
Windows NT	PagePlus	MSN UK
Main Office Applications	Paint Shop Pro	Netscape Communicator
Access	Photoshop	Web Page Design
Excel	Publisher	**Development Tools**
Microsoft Office 97	QuarkXPress	Delphi
Microsoft Office	**Accounting and Finance**	Java Applets
Microsoft Office SBE	Microsoft Money UK	JavaScript
Microsoft Outlook (98)	QuickBooks UK	Visual Basic
Microsoft Project	Quicken UK	Visual C++

Web: http://www.computerstep.com

Tel: +44 (0)1926 817999   Fax: +44 (0)1926 817005   Email: books@computerstep.com

EXCEL
in easy steps

Stephen Copestake

In easy steps is an imprint of Computer Step
Southfield Road . Southam
Warwickshire CV33 OFB . England

Tel: 01926 817999 Fax: 01926 817005
http://www.computerstep.com

Reprinted 1999, 1998
Second edition published 1997
First edition published 1996

Printed and bound in the United Kingdom

ISBN 1-874029-69-5

Contents

Getting started

In this chapter, you'll learn about the elements of the Excel screen, and about indispensable Excel terminology. You'll also discover how to use and customise toolbars, and how to enter data. You'll navigate through – and between – Excel worksheets, and become proficient in various selection techniques. Finally, you'll learn how to use Excel's comprehensive HELP system, including the Office Assistant.

Chapter One

Covers

The Excel screen – an overview

To start Excel, click the Start button in the Windows Task Bar, then Programs, Microsoft Excel. The opening screen will look like this:

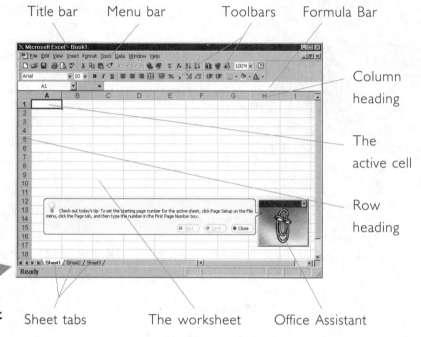

Title bar   Menu bar   Toolbars   Formula Bar

Column heading

The active cell

Row heading

Sheet tabs   The worksheet   Office Assistant

Hiding screen components

Some of the above components – e.g. the Formula Bar – can be removed from the screen, if required.

Pull down the Tools menu and click Options. Do the following:

1 Click this tab

2 Select or deselect any component(s)

3 Click this tab

Screen components in detail (1)

Cells occur where rows and columns intersect.

For a more detailed definition of worksheets and workbooks, see page 13.

Components shown in the opening screen on page 8 are explained in more detail now:

The worksheet

This is the large central rectangular area which is subdivided into a grid of cells. The cells are used to store data.

The Title Bar

The Title Bar contains the program title and the name of the overall Excel workbook. It also contains (at the left-hand end) the button for the pull-down control menu.

Remember that the easiest way to exit from Excel is to double-click this button with the left-hand mouse button.

The Menu Bar

This contains menu titles for all the commands used to build, format and control Excel worksheets. Clicking any title with the left mouse button will display a pull-down menu from which various options may be selected.

Toolbars

Toolbars are collections of icons representing the most commonly used commands required for standard tasks. By clicking an icon, you initiate the command. This represents a major saving in time and effort.

Excel 97 comes with 13 toolbars, of which some of the most commonly used are:

- Standard

- Formatting

- Web

See pages 11-12 for how to customise and work with toolbars.

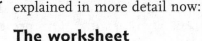

Screen components in detail (2)

The Formula Bar

This displays the location and contents of the currently selected cell. The Formula Bar represents a particularly useful way to enter:

- formulas

- other cell data (e.g. text)

Column headings

Column headings define each cell within a given column horizontally. Columns are labelled A, B, C, etc.

Row headings

Row headings define each cell within a given row vertically. Rows are numbered 1, 2, 3, etc.

REMEMBER

For how to use the vertical and horizontal scroll bars to navigate through Excel worksheets, see page 18.

The Vertical Scroll Bar

This enables you to move the visible window vertically up and down the worksheet, under the control of the mouse.

The Horizontal Scroll Bar

This enables you to move the visible window horizontally to the left or right across the worksheet.

Sheet tabs

These enable you to select which spreadsheet should be displayed. By clicking on a sheet tab, you jump to the relevant sheet.

The Office Assistant

The Office Assistant is an interactive source of help. See pages 22-24 for how to use it.

Working with toolbars (1)

Toolbars are important components in Excel. A toolbar is an on-screen bar which contains shortcut buttons. These symbolise and allow easy access to often-used commands which would normally have to be invoked via one or more menus.

For example, Excel's Standard toolbar lets you:

- create, open, save and print documents

- perform copy & paste and cut & paste operations

- undo editing actions

- access Excel's HELP system

by simply clicking on the relevant button.

You can control which toolbars display.

Specifying which toolbars are visible

Pull down the View menu and click Toolbars. Now do the following:

To strip the screen so it contains only the Menu bar and Row/Column headings (a technique which makes it easier to work with large worksheets), pull down the View menu and click Full Screen.

To return to the normal view, do the following:

Click here

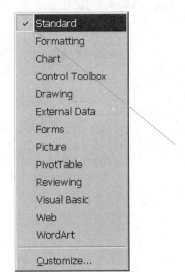

Click the toolbar you want to be visible – a ✔ appears against it

Repeat this procedure for as many toolbars as necessary.

Working with toolbars (2)

Adding buttons to toolbars

By default, the pre-defined toolbars which come with Excel have only a small number of buttons associated with them. However, just about all editing operations you can perform from within Excel menus can be incorporated as a button within the toolbar of your choice, for convenience and ease of access.

To do this, first make sure the toolbar you want to add one or more buttons to is visible (see page 11 for how to do this). Move the mouse pointer over the toolbar and right-click once. In the menu which appears, click Customize. Now do the following:

Ensure this tab is active

REMEMBER

Repeat steps 2 to 4 as often as necessary.

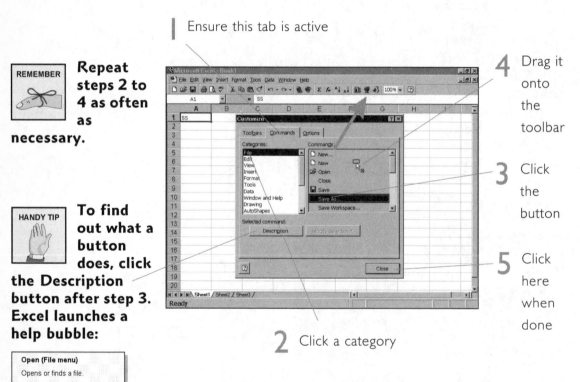

4 Drag it onto the toolbar

3 Click the button

5 Click here when done

2 Click a category

HANDY TIP

To find out what a button does, click the Description button after step 3. Excel launches a help bubble:

Open (File menu)
Opens or finds a file.

Press Esc to clear it.

Basic terminology (1)

Here, we explore some of the basic terms used throughout Excel.

Worksheets

'Worksheet' is Excel's name for a spreadsheet. Worksheets are arrays of cells used to store data. This often involves simple arithmetical calculations linking the cells together in tables, usually for some kind of analysis.

Worksheets are the essential building-blocks of workbooks – see below.

 By default, Excel workbooks contain 3 worksheets (*Sheet 1*, *Sheet 2* and *Sheet 3*).

Workbooks

A workbook is a file which holds together a collection of worksheets (and possibly charts – for more information on charts, see Chapter 13). It will be seen in later chapters that it is usual to have several worksheets linked together and often convenient to summarise the data on these worksheets in the form of associated charts or graphs.

 See Chapter 4 for more information on workbooks.

When you create a new document in Excel, you're actually creating a new workbook. Each new workbook has a default name: *Book 1*, *Book 2* etc.

The Worksheet Window

The opening Excel window displays (typically):

- 9 columns labelled A to I

- 18 rows labelled 1 to 18

The exact number of rows and columns shown depends on the screen size, video driver and resolution.

It must be appreciated that this is only the extreme top left-hand corner of the full worksheet which extends to:

 This means each worksheet contains 16,777,216 cells.

- 256 columns labelled A to Z then AA to IV

- 65,536 rows labelled 1 to 65,536

See the illustration on page 14 for further clarification.

Basic terminology (2)

This area covers the cell range A1 to I18.

As we've just seen, the Excel screen displays only a tiny section of the available worksheet. The illustration below displays this graphically:

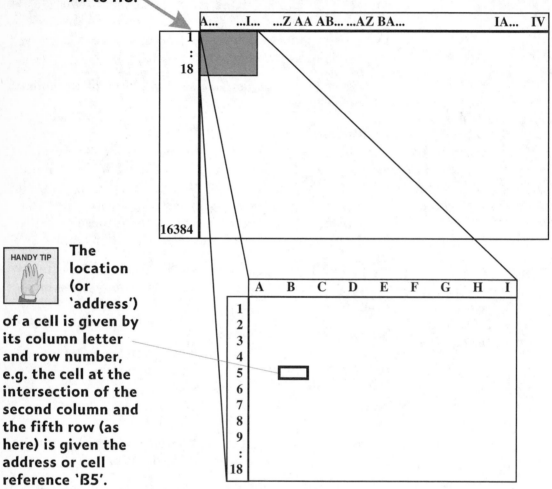

The location (or 'address') of a cell is given by its column letter and row number, e.g. the cell at the intersection of the second column and the fifth row (as here) is given the address or cell reference 'B5'.

The grey section – only a tiny part of the overall worksheet – is shown in magnified form in the lower half of the illustration.

Keying in data (1)

In Excel, you can enter the following basic data types:

- values (i.e. numbers)

- text (e.g. headings and explanatory material)

- functions (e.g. Sine or Cosine)

- formulas (combinations of values, text and functions)

You can use two techniques to enter data into any cell in a worksheet.

Entering data directly

First, move the mouse pointer over any cell and left-click once. Alternatively, you can also use the keyboard to target a cell: simply move the cell pointer with the cursor keys until it's over the relevant cell.

Whichever method you use, Excel surrounds the active cell with a border.

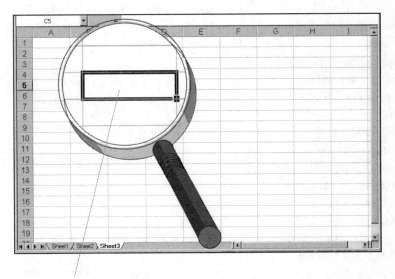

Magnified view of
active cell

Keying in data (2)

Now begin to key in the information required. It will appear simultaneously in the cell and in the Formula Bar.

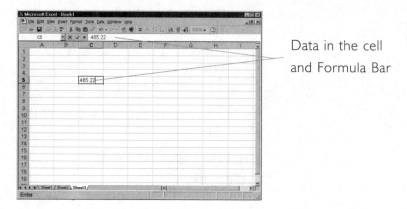

Data in the cell and Formula Bar

HANDY TIP

When you enter values which are too big (physically) to fit in the holding cell, Excel inserts:

#####

To resolve this, widen the column (see page 35 for how to do this). Or pull down the Format menu and click Column, Autofit Selection (to have Excel automatically increase the column size to match the contents).

Finally, press Enter to confirm entry of the data (or Esc to cancel the operation).

Entering data via the Formula bar

Click the cell you want to insert data into. Then click the Formula Bar. Type in the data. Then follow step 1 below. If you decide not to proceed with the operation, follow step 2 instead:

Click here to confirm the operation

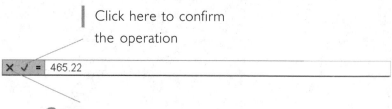

2 Click here to cancel the operation

Selection techniques

Groups of adjacent cells are known as 'ranges' in Excel.

Ranges are described in terms of their upper-left and lower-right cell references (with each separated by a colon).

For example, the range beginning with cell D3 and ending with H16 would be shown as:

D3:H16

Non-adjacent ranges are separated by commas e.g.:

A3:B9,D3:H16

To select *all* cells within the current worksheet, do the following:

Click here

Excel operates by selection. In other words, you have to select one or more cells before you can work with them. On page 15, we saw how to target – and enter data into – one specific cell. Here, we'll examine ways to select multiple cells.

Selecting multiple adjacent cells

Click in one corner of the cells you want to select. Hold down the left mouse button and drag to the far corner.

A selected cell range

Selecting multiple cell ranges

Hold down one Ctrl key as you use the above technique.

Selecting rows

To select a single row, click the row heading. To select more than one row, hold down one Ctrl key as you click multiple row headings.

Selecting columns

To select a single column, click the column heading. To select more than one column, hold down one Ctrl key as you click multiple column headings.

Row headings   Column headings

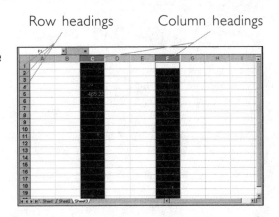

Two columns selected

Moving around in worksheets (1)

Excel worksheets are huge. Moving to cells which happen to be visible is easy: you simply click in the relevant cell. However, Excel provides several techniques you can use to jump to less accessible areas.

Using the scroll bars

Use any of the following methods:

HANDY TIP

Re step 1 – holding down one Shift key as you drag the scroll box speeds up the operation dramatically.

1.   to scroll quickly to another section of the active worksheet, drag the scroll box along the scroll bar until you reach it

2.   to move one window to the right or left, click to the left or right of the scroll box in the horizontal scroll bar

HANDY TIP

When you carry out steps 1 and 2 on the right, Excel displays a bubble showing where you're up to:

Row: 13

3.   to move one window up or down, click above or below the scroll box in the vertical scroll bar

4.   to move up or down by one row, click the arrows in the vertical scroll bar

5.   to move left or right by one column, click the arrows in the horizontal scroll bar

Scroll boxes

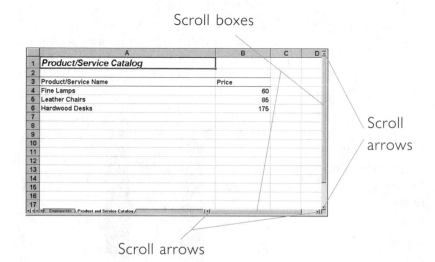

Scroll arrows

Scroll arrows

Moving around in worksheets (2)

HANDY TIP

Excel facilitates worksheet navigation. As you move the insertion point from cell to cell, the relevant row and column headers are emboldened:

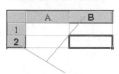

Illuminated headers

HANDY TIP

You can use a keyboard shortcut to launch the Go To dialog: simply press F5, or Ctrl+G.

REMEMBER

Re step 1 – a cell's 'reference' (or 'address') identifies it in relation to its position in a worksheet, e.g. BII or H23. You can also type in cell ranges here.

Using the keyboard

You can use the following techniques:

1.   use the cursor keys to move one cell left, right, up or down.

2.   hold down Ctrl as you use step 1 above; this jumps to the edge of the current section (e.g. if cell BII is active and you hold down Ctrl as you press ➔, Excel jumps to IVII, the last cell in row II).

3.   press Home to jump to the first cell in the active row, or Ctrl+Home to move to AI.

4.   press Page Up or Page Down to move up or down by one screen.

5.   press Alt+Page Down to move one screen to the right, or Alt+Page Up to move one screen to the left.

Using the Go To dialog

Excel provides a special dialog which you can use to specify precise cell destinations.

Pull down the Edit menu and click Go To. Now do the following:

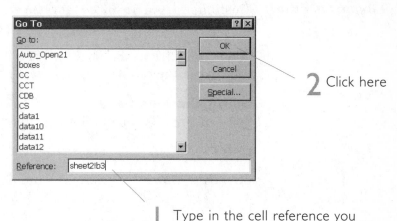

2 Click here

Type in the cell reference you want to move to

Switching between worksheets

Because workbooks have more than one worksheet, Excel provides two easy and convenient methods for moving between them.

Using the Tab area

You can use the Tab area (at the base of the Excel screen) to:

- jump to the first or last sheet

- jump to the next or previous sheet

- jump to a specific sheet

HANDY TIP

The worksheets shown here have been given customised names. To do this, double-click the relevant sheet entry in the Tab area. Amend the default name appropriately. Finally, press Enter.

See the illustration below:

To first sheet   To next sheet

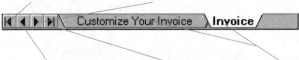

To previous sheet   To last sheet   Customised sheet tabs

To move to a specific sheet, simply click the relevant tab.

An example: in the illustration above, to jump to the 'Customize Your Invoice' worksheet, simply click the appropriate tab.

When you click a worksheet tab, Excel emboldens the name and makes the tab background white.

Using the keyboard

You can use a keyboard shortcut here.

Ctrl+Page Up   moves to the previous tab

Ctrl+Page Down   moves to the next tab

Using Excel's HELP system

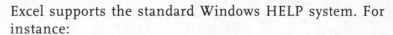

Excel supports the standard Windows HELP system. For instance:

 Excel calls these highly specific HELP bubbles 'ToolTips'. ToolTips are a specialised form of ScreenTips (see below).

- moving the mouse pointer over toolbar buttons produces an explanatory HELP bubble:

Excel calls these highly specific HELP topics 'ScreenTips'.

- moving the mouse pointer over fields in dialogs, commands or screen areas and right-clicking produces a specific help box. Carry out the following procedure to activate this.

Left-click here for the specific help topic

If you have a suitable browser (e.g. Internet Explorer), a modem and an account with a service provider, you can also access Excel-specific Internet help.
  Ensure your connection is live. Pull down the Help menu and click Microsoft on the Web. In the sub-menu, click the relevant option.

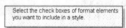

Other standard Windows HELP features are also present – see your Windows documentation for how to use these.

An additional HELP feature, introduced in Excel 97, is the Office Assistant. See the next topic.

The Office Assistant (1)

The Office Assistant, a unique HELP feature introduced in Excel 97, is designed to make it much easier to become productive. The Office Assistant:

- answers questions directly. This is an especially useful feature for the reason that, normally when you invoke a program's HELP system, you know more or less the question you want to ask, or the topic on which you need information. If neither of these is true, however, Office Assistant responds to plain English questions and provides a choice of answers. For example, responses produced by entering 'What are ToolTips?' include:

— Show or hide shortcut keys in ToolTips

— Show or hide toolbar ScreenTips

— Turn ScreenTips off

- provides context-sensitive tips

- offers HELP which relates specifically to the latest version of Excel

HANDY TIP

**The Office Assistant is animated. It can also change shape! To do this, click the Options button:
In the dialog which appears, activate the Gallery tab. Click the Next button until the Assistant you want is displayed. Then click OK.**

The Office Assistant, after it has just launched

HANDY TIP

If the Assistant HELP bubble isn't displayed, simply click anywhere in the Assistant.

The Office Assistant (2)

 If the Office Assistant isn't on-screen when a tip is launched, the toolbar button which launches it changes to:

Launching the Office Assistant

By default, the Office Assistant displays automatically. If it isn't currently on-screen, however, refer to the Standard toolbar and do the following:

Click here

 The bulb denotes a latent tip

Displaying tips

Ensure the Office Assistant is on-screen. Then do the following:

 Sometimes, the Office Assistant itself will indicate that it has a tip which may be useful:

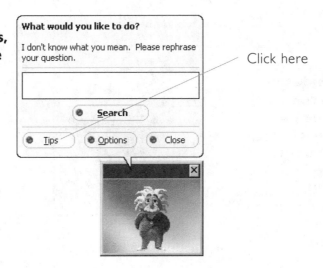

What would you like to do?

I don't know what you mean. Please rephrase your question.

Click here

Search

Tips   Options   Close

Click here to view a suggested tip

A context-sensitive tip appears. Do the following when you've finished with it:

 Click Next or Back (if available) to view another tip:

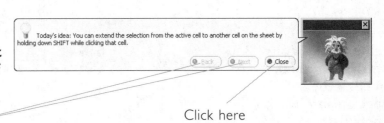

Today's idea: You can extend the selection from the active cell to another cell on the sheet by holding down SHIFT while clicking that cell.

Back   Next   Close

Click here

The Office Assistant (3)

Previous versions of Excel had a feature called the Answer Wizard. This allowed you to enter questions in plain English. The advantage of using the Answer Wizard was that you could use it to find information on topics which you weren't sure how to classify.

The Office Assistant incorporates an improved version of the Answer Wizard.

Asking questions

First, ensure the Office Assistant is visible. Then do the following:

HANDY TIP

To close an Office Assistant window at any time, press Esc. Or click the Close button:

HANDY TIP

To hide the Office Assistant, right-click it. In the menu, click Hide Assistant.

REMEMBER

Re step 3 – if none of the topics are suitable, click See More (if available). Then click the correct option in the new list.

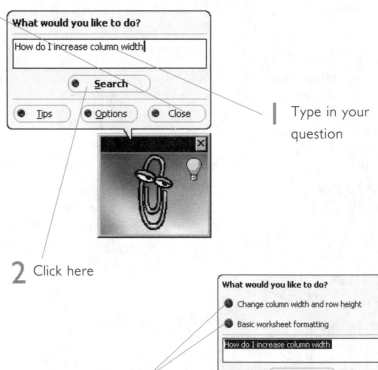

Type in your question

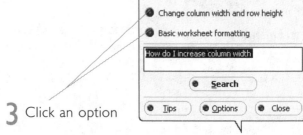

2 Click here

3 Click an option

Worksheet basics

Chapter Two

In this chapter, you'll learn how to 'forward-plan' worksheets, to ensure your data is easy to follow. We'll also examine the different types of data you can enter, and look at how to modify data you've already entered. Excel has several features which act as shortcuts to data entry; you'll learn how to use these to save time and effort. Then you'll discover how to work with number formats, insert formulas into cells and carry out simple What-If tests. Finally, you'll resize rows and columns, and insert new cells, rows and columns.

Covers

Layout planning

When you start Excel, a blank worksheet is automatically created and loaded. This means you can click any cell and start entering data immediately. However, it's a good idea to give some thought to an overall layout strategy before you do this.

Look at the simple worksheet excerpt below:

2	Widgets ordered =	425
3	Price per unit =	0.73
4	Amount due (excluding VAT) =	

HANDY TIP

As you enter data into your worksheet, use the techniques discussed here (and on page 35) to ensure your data is clear and easily comprehensible.
   You should also ensure your worksheet has an effective overall 'look' – see Chapter 11 for more information on how to format worksheets.

Here, the text occupies far more space than the numbers and formulas. The problem has been solved by widening the column containing the text (see page 35 for how to do this). The problem is that this method prevents subsequent lines in the column from being subdivided into further columns.

Look at the next illustration:

2	Widgets ordered =	425
3	Price per unit =	0.73
4	Amount due (excluding VAT) =	

This text has bled into the next column

Here, on the other hand, the final text entry has been allowed to straddle as many adjacent columns as necessary. The proviso here is that you must ensure you leave as many empty adjacent cells as are necessary fully to display the text.

HANDY TIP

The second method is often the most flexible.

Data types

HANDY TIP

To force a sequence of digits to be input as text, precede them by a single quote.
  For instance, to type in 1234 as text type: `'1234`.

In Chapter 1 (pages 15-16), we looked at how to key in simple data. Now, we'll examine the types of data you can enter in more detail.

Excel determines the type of data entered into a cell by the sequence of characters keyed. The types are:

- Numbers (i.e. digits, decimal point, #, %, +, −)

- Text (any other string of characters)

- Formulas (always preceded by =)

The worksheet excerpt below shows these data types in action:

REMEMBER

These are default alignments. To apply a new alignment, select the cell(s). Right-click over them. In the menu, click Format Cells. In the Format Cells dialog, click the Alignment tab. Select a new alignment/ orientation. Click OK.

B2 contains text (aligned to the left of the cell)

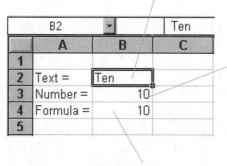

B3 contains the number 10 (aligned to the right of the cell)

B4 contains the hidden formula: =6+4

HANDY TIP

If you want to display the underlying formula rather than the result, select the relevant cell and press Ctrl+`.
  Note: the ` character is at the top left of the keyboard (below the function keys).

When a formula has been inserted into a cell, Excel evaluates it; the resultant value – in the case of B4 above, '10' – is shown (aligned to the right).

For more information on formulas, see pages 32-33.

Modifying existing data

HANDY TIP

Excel supports multiple undos and redos. To undo one or more editing actions, do the following:

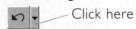 Click here

in the Standard toolbar. Make your selection in the list and press Enter. To redo one or more actions, do the following:

 Click here

in the Standard toolbar. Make your selection in the list and press Enter.

You can amend the contents of a cell in two ways:

* via the Formula bar

* from within the cell

When you use either of these methods, Excel enters a special state known as Edit Mode.

Amending existing data using the Formula Bar

Click the cell whose contents you want to change. Then click in the Formula bar. Make the appropriate revisions and/or additions. Then press Return. Excel updates the relevant cell.

Amending existing data internally

Click the cell whose contents you want to change. Press F2. Make the appropriate revisions and/or additions *within the cell*. Then press Return.

The illustration below shows a section of a workbook created with the template INVOICE.XLT supplied with Excel.

HANDY TIP

If direct editing doesn't work, pull down the Tools menu and click Options. Select the Edit tab, then click 'Edit directly in cell'. Finally, click OK.

A magnified view of cell K18, in Edit Mode

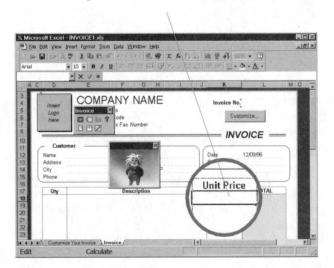

AutoComplete

Excel has a range of features which save you time and effort:

- AutoComplete

- AutoFill

- AutoCorrect

AutoComplete examines the contents of the active column and tries to anticipate what you're about to type. Look at the next illustration:

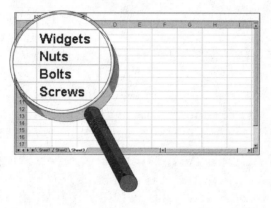

HANDY TIP

You can also use another technique. Instead of starting to type in the repeat entry, right-click over the cell. In the menu, click Pick From List. Now do the following:

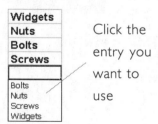

Click the entry you want to use

Here, we've entered a series of text values into cells B4:B7. If you want to duplicate any of these entries in B8, you can simply type in the first letter then press Enter.

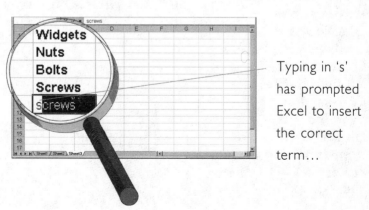

Typing in 's' has prompted Excel to insert the correct term...

AutoFill

Types of series you can use AutoFill to complete include:

- 1st Period, 2nd Period etc.
- Mon, Tue, Wed etc.
- Quarter 1, Quarter 2 etc.
- Week1, Week2, Week 3 etc.

Excel replaces some words/ phrases automatically as you type (e.g. 'accross' becomes 'across'). This is called AutoCorrect. To add your own substitutions, pull down the Tools menu and click AutoCorrect. In the Replace field in the AutoCorrect dialog, insert the *incorrect* word; in the With field, type in the *correct* version. Click OK.

Excel lets you insert data series automatically. This is a very useful and time-saving feature. Look at the illustration below:

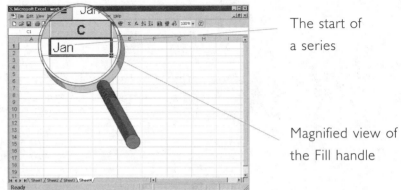

The start of a series

Magnified view of the Fill handle

If you wanted to insert month names in successive cells in column A, you could do so manually. But there's a much easier way. You can use Excel's AutoFill feature.

Using AutoFill to create a series

Type in the first element(s) of the series in consecutive cells. Select the cells. Then position the mouse pointer over the Fill handle in the bottom right-hand corner of the last cell (the pointer changes to a crosshair). Hold down the left mouse button and drag the handle over the cells into which you want to extend the series (in the example here, over C2:C12). When you release the mouse button, Excel extrapolates the initial entry or entries into the appropriate series.

The completed series

Number formats

REMEMBER

You can have Excel 'validate' data inserted into cells. This means that you can specify acceptable data types (i.e. data outside the criteria you impose will be unacceptable).

Select one or more cells. Pull down the Data menu and click Validation. In the Data Validation dialog, click the Settings tab. In the Allow field, select a validation type; complete the rest of the fields (they vary according to the type selected). Finally, click OK.

REMEMBER

Re step 3 – the options you can choose from vary according to the category chosen. Complete them as necessary.

You can customise the way cell contents (e.g. numbers and dates/times) display in Excel. You can specify:

- at what point numbers are rounded up

- how minus values are displayed (for example, whether they display in red, and/or with '–' in front of them)

- (in the case of currency values) which currency symbol (e.g. £ or $) is used

- (in the case of dates and times) the generic display type (e.g. *day/month/year* or *month/year*)

Available formats are organised under general categories. These include: Number, Currency and Fraction.

Specifying a number format

Select the cells whose contents you want to customise. Pull down the Format menu and click Cells. Now do the following:

Ensure the Number tab is active

3 Complete the relevant options

4 Click here

2 Click a category

Formulas – an overview

For brief details of frequently used formulas, do the following.

Pull down the Help menu and click Contents and Index. In the Help Topics... dialog, click the Index tab. In field 1, type:

formulas, examples

(make sure you type in the separating space). Then click the Display button.

When you've finished using the formula list, press Esc.

REMEMBER

You can enter Internet addresses in formulas.

Use the following as a guide:

=[http://www.anypage/ workbook.xls]Sheet9!C3

In other words, enclose the address and workbook name in square brackets. Separate the sheet name and cell range with !

Formulas are cell entries which define how other values relate to each other.

As a very simple example, consider the following:

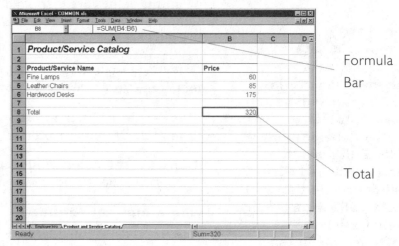

Formula Bar

Total

Here, a cell has been defined which returns the total of cells B4:B6. Obviously, in this instance you could insert the total easily enough yourself because the individual values are so small, and because we're only dealing with a small number of cells. But what happens if the cell values are larger and/or more numerous, or – more to the point – if they're liable to change frequently?

The answer is to insert a formula which carries out the necessary calculation automatically.

If you look at the Formula bar in the illustration, you'll see the formula which does this:

=SUM(B4:B6)

Many Excel formulas are much more complex than this, but the principles remain the same.

Inserting a formula

Arguments (e.g. cell references) relating to functions are always contained in brackets.

To enter the same formula into a cell range, select the range, type the formula and then press Ctrl+Enter.

If you want to revise a formula, you can also use a feature known as Range Finder.

Double-click the cell which contains the formula; Excel applies a separate colour to each cell range referred to in the formula. Drag the relevant coloured border to restate the formula reference (or drag the border handle to extend or reduce it).

Finally, press Enter.

All formulas in Excel begin with an equals sign. This is usually followed by a permutation of the following:

- an operand (cell reference, e.g. B4)

- a function (e.g. the summation function, SUM)

- an arithmetical operator (+, −, / and *)

- comparison operators (<, >, <=, >= and =)

Excel supports a very wide range of functions organised into numerous categories. For more information on how to insert functions, see Chapter 6.

The mathematical operators are (in the order in which they appear in the bulleted list): *plus*, *minus*, *divide* and *multiply*.

The comparison operators are (in the order in which they appear in the list): *less than*, *greater than*, *less than or equal to*, *greater than or equal to* and *equals*.

There are two ways to enter or amend formulas:

Directly into the cell

Click the cell in which you want to insert a formula. Then type =, followed by your formula. When you've finished, press Return.

Via the Formula bar

This is usually the most convenient method.

Click the cell in which you want to insert a formula. Then click in the Formula Bar. Type =, followed by your formula. When you've finished, press Return or do the following:

Click here

Simple What-If tests

The power of a worksheet is only really appreciated when you carry out 'What-If' tests. These involve adjusting the numbers in selected cells in order to observe the effect on formulas throughout the worksheet. Any such changes 'ripple through' the worksheet.

In the simple example below, C4 has the following formula:

$=c2*c3$

which multiplies the contents of C2 by C3.

	A	B	C
1			
2		Widgets ordered =	425
3		Price per unit =	0.73
4		Amount due (excluding VAT) =	310.25

HANDY TIP

If changes you make to data don't produce the relevant update, pull down the Tools menu and click Options. In the Options dialog, select the Calculation tab. Click Automatic in the Calculation section, followed by OK.

By entering alternative values into C2 or C3, you can watch the changes filter through to C4. In the next illustration, the value in C2 has changed; Excel has automatically calculated the effect on the total:

	A	B	C
1			
2		Widgets ordered =	562
3		Price per unit =	0.73
4		Amount due (excluding VAT) =	410.26

The change in C2 has automatically adjusted the C4 total

Amending row/column sizes

Sooner or later, you'll find it necessary to change the width of rows or columns. This necessity arises when there is too much data in cells to display adequately. You can enlarge or shrink single or multiple rows/columns.

Changing row height

To change one row's height, click the row heading. If you want to change multiple rows, hold down Ctrl and click the appropriate extra headings. Then place the mouse pointer over the line located just under the row heading(s). Hold down the left mouse button and drag the line up or down to decrease or increase the row(s) respectively. Release the mouse button to confirm the operation.

Excel has a useful 'best fit' feature. Simply double-click the line below the selected row headings, or to the right of selected column headings, to have the rows or columns adjust themselves automatically to their contents.

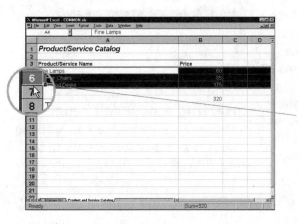

A magnified view of the line to drag if you're amending rows 4, 5 and 6 jointly

Changing column width

To change one column's width, click the column heading. If you want to change multiple columns, hold down Ctrl and click the appropriate extra headings. Then place the mouse pointer over the line located just to the right of the column heading(s). Hold down the left mouse button and drag the line right or left to widen or narrow the column(s) respectively.

Release the mouse button to confirm the operation.

Inserting cells, rows or columns

You can insert additional cells, rows or columns into worksheets.

REMEMBER

If you select cells in more than one row or column, Excel inserts the equivalent number of new rows or columns.

Inserting a new row or column

First, select one or more cells within the row(s) or column(s) where you want to carry out the insert operation. Now pull down the Insert menu and click Rows or Columns, as appropriate. Excel inserts the new row(s) or column(s) immediately.

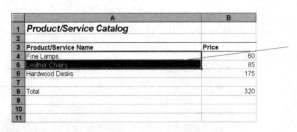

A worksheet extract. Here, one new column or two new rows are being added

REMEMBER

To delete 1 or more rows or columns, select the heading(s). Right-click over the rows/columns; select Delete from the menu.

Inserting a new cell range

Select the range where you want to insert the new cells. Pull down the Insert menu and click Cells. Now carry out step 1 or step 2 below. Finally, follow step 3.

1 Click here to have Excel make room for the new cells by moving the selected range *to the right*

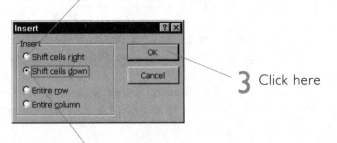

3 Click here

BEWARE

If you delete rows or columns, be careful you don't delete cells which are needed (e.g. those referred to in formulas, or containing data in a part of the row/column which is currently invisible).

2 Click here to have Excel make room for the new cells by moving the selected range *down*

Copy/move techniques

In this chapter, you'll learn now to copy and move cells. You'll copy data within the host worksheet, to another worksheet and to another (open) workbook. You'll also perform copy operations which are restricted to specific cell aspects, then make use of a shortcut which makes copying data to *adjacent* cells even easier. Finally, you'll move worksheets to a different location within the host workbook, and to another workbook.

Covers

Chapter Three

Copying and moving cells

Excel lets you copy or move cells:

- within the same worksheet

- from one worksheet to another

- from one worksheet to another worksheet in a different workbook

When you copy or move data in cells which contain formulas, Excel adjusts the cell references appropriately.

Copying data within the same worksheet

Select the cell range which contains the data you want to copy. Move the mouse pointer over the range border; it changes to an arrow. Hold down one Ctrl key; left-click and drag the range to the new location. Release the mouse button.

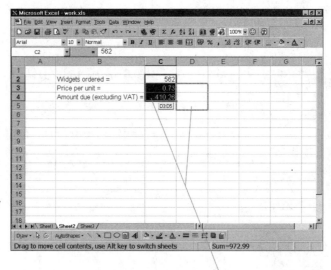

You can use another method to copy or move cell data.

Select the data. Press Ctrl+C to copy it, or Ctrl+X to move it. Position the cursor where you want the copied/moved data inserted. Press Ctrl+V or Shift+Insert.

Cells in the course of being copied

Moving data within the same worksheet

Select the cell range which contains the data you want to move. Place the mouse pointer over the range border; it changes to an arrow. Left-click and drag the range to the new location. Release the mouse button.

Advanced copying

Excel lets you be highly specific about which cell components are copied. You can use a special technique to limit the copy/move operation to any of the following:

The techniques discussed on this page only apply to *copy* operations.

- the cell format

- underlying formulas

- cell values

- any data validation rules you've set

- all cell contents and formats with the exception of borders

Performing specific copy operations

Select the data you want to copy. Then refer to the Standard toolbar and do the following:

Click here

Don't press Enter after carrying out step 2.
If you do, *all* cell components are copied to the Paste Area.

Click the upper left cell in the Paste Area (the cell range into which you want the data inserted). Pull down the Edit menu and click Paste Special. Now carry out the following steps:

Click the relevant option

Click Transpose – before you carry out step 2 – to have Excel change columns of copied data to rows (or vice versa).

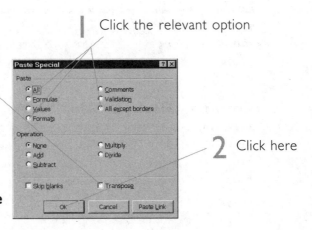

2 Click here

External copy/move operations

When you move the mouse pointer over the appropriate tab, Excel highlights it: Drag the cell range back into the worksheet area (the second worksheet is now displayed) and position the range in the correct location.

You can easily copy or move a range of cells between worksheets and workbooks.

Moving data to another Worksheet

Select the cell range which contains the data you want to move. Place the mouse pointer over the range border; it changes to an arrow. Hold down the Alt key; left-click and drag the range onto the relevant worksheet tab:

The Worksheet tab area at
the base of the screen

Release the mouse button.

Copying data to another Worksheet

Select the cell range which contains the data you want to copy. Place the mouse pointer over the range border; it changes to an arrow. Hold down the Alt key and one Ctrl key; left-click and drag the range onto the relevant worksheet tab, then position it using the techniques discussed in the Remember tip.

Moving data to another Workbook

First open both workbooks in separate windows (for how to do this, see your Windows documentation). Select the cell range which contains the data you want to move. Place the mouse pointer over the range border; it changes to an arrow. Left-click and drag the range onto the relevant worksheet in the second workbook.

Copying data to another Workbook

First open both workbooks in separate windows (for how to do this, see your Windows documentation). Select the cell range which contains the data you want to copy. Place the mouse pointer over the range border; it changes to an arrow. Hold down one Ctrl key; left-click and drag the range onto the relevant worksheet in the second workbook.

Entering data automatically

On page 30, we looked at the use of AutoFill to extrapolate data from one or more cells into additional cells. You can also use a variant of AutoFill to make copying data easier.

Copying data to adjacent cells – a shortcut

Select the cell range which contains the data you want to copy.

On page 30

BEWARE **If you don't hold down one Ctrl key as you drag, Excel will attempt to extrapolate rather than copy the data.**

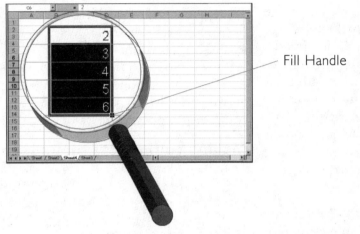

Fill Handle

BEWARE **Even if you do hold down a Ctrl key as you drag, Excel *may* still extrapolate the data. This occurs if you only selected 1 cell and this contains a simple value.**

In other words, if A3 contains '50' when you select it, holding down Ctrl and dragging the Fill Handle will insert values incremented by 1 (i.e. '51', '52', '53' etc.) in the flagged cells.

Move the mouse pointer over the Fill Handle. Hold down one Ctrl key; left-click and drag the handle over as many adjacent cells as you want to copy the data into:

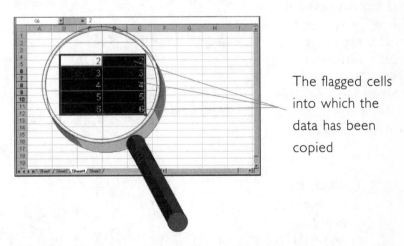

The flagged cells into which the data has been copied

Release the mouse pointer to confirm the copy operation.

Moving worksheets

HANDY TIP

To insert a new worksheet, click the tab (in the tab area) which represents the sheet in front of which you want the new worksheet inserted. (To insert multiple sheets, hold down Shift and click the relevant number of tabs.)
Finally, pull down the Insert menu and click Worksheet.

You can perform two kinds of move operation on worksheets. You can:

* rearrange the worksheet order within a given workbook

* transfer a worksheet to another workbook

Rearranging worksheets

To select a single worksheet, click the relevant sheet tab in the worksheet tab area. Or select more than one worksheet by holding down one Shift key as you click multiple tabs. With the mouse pointer still over the selected tab(s), hold down the left mouse button and drag them to their new location in the tab area. Release the mouse button to confirm the operation.

Moving worksheets to another workbook

To select a single worksheet, click the relevant sheet tab in the worksheet tab area. Or select more than one worksheet by holding down one Shift key as you click multiple tabs. Pull down the Edit menu and click Move or Copy Sheet. Now do the following:

HANDY TIP

To delete a worksheet, click its tab in the tab area. Pull down the Edit menu and click Delete Sheet. In the message which launches, click OK.
Note that deleting a sheet erases its contents, too!

Click here; select the new host workbook from the drop-down list

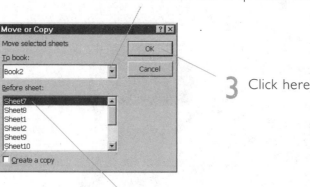

3 Click here

HANDY TIP

Click here to perform a copy operation rather than a move.

2 Click the worksheet in front of which you want the transferred sheet(s) to appear

Workbook management

In this chapter, you'll learn how to create new workbooks. Once created, workbooks need to be saved to disk and reopened. You'll also discover how to save workbooks as templates (for later use as the basis of workbook creation) and as HTML files (for use on the World Wide Web). You'll use an Excel Add-In – AutoSave – to have Excel save your work automatically, at an interval you set. Finally, you'll save (and reopen) your overall environment as a workspace, and then close all active workbooks.

Chapter Four

Covers

Creating new workbooks

Creating new workbooks is made easy by the provision of templates. A template is a pre-designed workbook which is ready to use. The templates supplied with Excel contain:

- numerous pre-defined fields

- several pre-defined worksheets

- pre-defined formatting

- special buttons which you can click to launch features directly

As well as using the templates provided, you can design your own – see page 46. Alternatively you can create a new blank worksheet – see the Handy Tip on the left.

Creating a workbook

Pull down the File menu and click New. Now do the following:

HANDY TIP **Re step 1 – to create a new *blank* workbook,** activate the *General* tab. Then omit steps 2 and 3; instead, double-click this icon:

in the New dialog. Excel creates a new workbook (with 3 blank worksheets).

Activate this tab

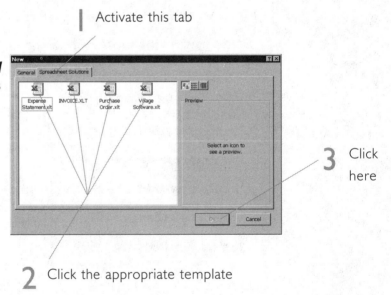

3 Click here

2 Click the appropriate template

Saving new workbooks

It's important to save your work at frequent intervals, in order to avoid data loss in the event of a hardware fault or power interruption. Carry out the following procedure:

Saving a workbook for the first time

Pull down the File menu and click Save. Or press Ctrl+S. Now do the following:

REMEMBER

The procedures listed here assume the new workbook is being saved to disk for the first time.

If this isn't the case, see 'Saving existing workbooks' below.

2 Click here. In the drop-down list, click the drive you want to host the workbook

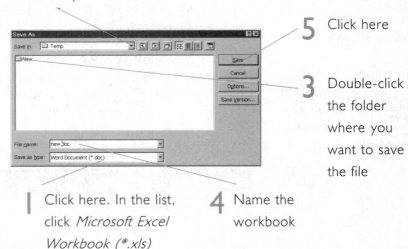

5 Click here

3 Double-click the folder where you want to save the file

1 Click here. In the list, click *Microsoft Excel Workbook (*.xls)*

4 Name the workbook

Saving existing workbooks

Pull down the File menu and click Save. Alternatively, refer to the Standard toolbar and do the following:

REMEMBER

If the file hasn't been saved before, then the Save As dialogue box will be displayed.

See 'Saving a workbook for the first time' above for how to use this.

Click here

Saving workbooks as templates

Workbooks you've created and formatted can be saved as templates, for future use. When you've done this, you can base new documents on them, a considerable saving in time and effort. For how to do this, see page 44.

By default, workbook templates are saved to the following folder:

\PROGRAM FILES\MICROSOFT OFFICE\TEMPLATES

and appear as icons in the New dialog. You may wish, however, to save Excel templates to the Spreadsheet Solutions folder – see below.

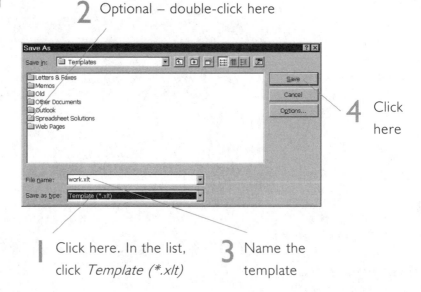

REMEMBER

Excel templates have the following suffix:

.XLT

Saving a workbook as a template

Pull down the File menu and click Save As. Carry out the following steps:

2 Optional – double-click here

4 Click here

1 Click here. In the list, click *Template (*.xlt)*

3 Name the template

Saving to the Internet

Re step 2 – to publish your Office documents on the Web, you must have access to the Internet (e.g. via a service provider), and you must have installed a modem. For help with step 2, consult your service provider. For more information on the Internet in general, read a companion volume: 'Internet UK in easy steps'.

You can save Excel workbooks to any HTTP site on the World Wide Web. This is a two-stage process:

1. saving your completed workbook in HTML (HyperText Markup Language) format

2. copying the HTML files to your service provider

Step 2 is outside the scope of this book.

Pull down the File menu and click Save as HTML. Excel now launches the Internet Assistant Wizard. This consists of 4 dialogs. The first is shown below. Do the following:

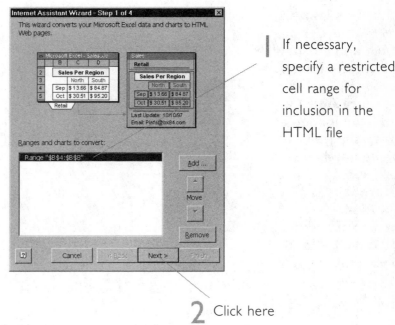

If necessary, specify a restricted cell range for inclusion in the HTML file

2 Click here

REMEMBER

You can use the Web toolbar to browse through or open any Web documents. For example: click ← to move backwards, → to move forwards. Click Favorites, Add to Favorites to add the current Web page to your list of often used sites...

Now complete the additional Wizard dialogs which appear (in each case, click the Next button to continue). Finally, do the following in the last dialog:

Click here

Other save operations

Additional formats you can save to include:

- **earlier versions of Excel**
- **various Microsoft Works formats**

Add-Ins are separate programs which add optional features to Excel. Optional, because the more Add-Ins you have loaded at once, the greater the demands on your system.

AutoSave is installed automatically, but you have to 'load' it to be able to use it.

Saving to other formats

Excel lets you save your workbooks to a variety of third-party formats. To do this, refer to page 45, then do the following:

In step 1, don't select *Microsoft Excel Workbook (*.xls)*; instead, click the relevant external format. Then carry out steps 2-5.

Using AutoSave

You can have Excel save workbooks automatically, at intervals you specify. This is a two-stage process.

If you haven't used AutoSave before, pull down the Tools menu and click Add-Ins. Do the following:

Click here

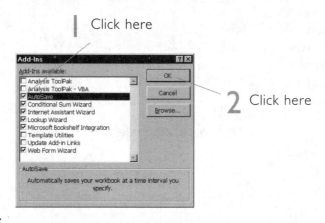

2 Click here

AutoSave is now loaded. Pull down the Tools menu and click AutoSave. Do the following:

Type in an AutoSave interval

2 Click here

Ensure this is selected to have Excel require your confirmation before any AutoSave operation.

Opening workbooks

HANDY TIP

Re step 4 – if you store workbooks in one folder, you can have Excel's Open dialog default to this.

Pull down the Tools menu and click Options. In the Options dialog, activate the General tab. In the Default file location field, type in the default folder e.g.:
C:\MYFILES
Finally, click OK.

When a new workbook has been saved, carry out the following procedure to open it:

Pull down the File menu and click Open. Now carry out the following steps:

3 Click here. In the drop-down list, click the drive that hosts the workbook

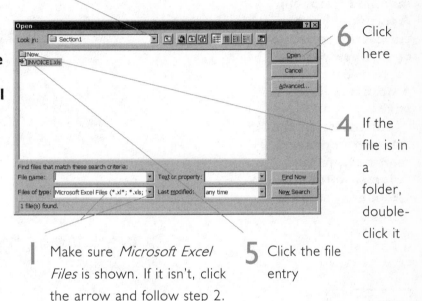

6 Click here

4 If the file is in a folder, double-click it

1 Make sure *Microsoft Excel Files* is shown. If it isn't, click the arrow and follow step 2.

5 Click the file entry

HANDY TIP

You can copy, rename or delete workbooks within the Open dialog.

Right-click any workbook entry. In the menu, click the desired option. Now carry out the appropriate action – e.g. to rename the workbook, type in the new name and press Enter.

2 Click here

Opening workbooks on the Internet

To open Internet workbooks, you must have access to the Internet (e.g. via a service provider), and you must have installed a modem. Additionally, your connection must be open when you carry out the procedures listed here.

(For advice on the Internet in general, read a companion volume: 'Internet UK in easy steps'.)

You can open workbooks stored at any HTTP site on the World Wide Web.

If the Web toolbar isn't currently on-screen, move the mouse pointer over any existing toolbar and right-click. In the menu which appears, click Web. Now do the following:

Click here

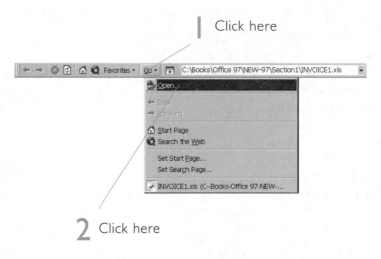

2 Click here

If you don't know the site address, don't follow step 3. Instead, click the Browse button. Use the Browse dialog (a variant of the Open dialog discussed on page 49) to locate it. Click Open. Then follow step 4.

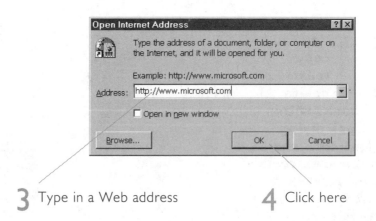

3 Type in a Web address

4 Click here

Using workspaces

Sometimes when you work with Excel, you'll require:

• more than one workbook open simultaneously

• multiple worksheets open simultaneously

Instead of having to open each component separately, you can save details of your current working environment as a 'workspace'. When you've done this, you can simply reopen the workspace; Excel then opens the constituent workbooks/worksheets for you.

Saving the current environment as a workspace

Pull down the File menu and click Save Workspace. Now carry out the following steps:

HANDY TIP

The default filename for a workspace is: RESUME.XLW.

2 Click here. In the drop-down list, click the drive you want to host the workspace

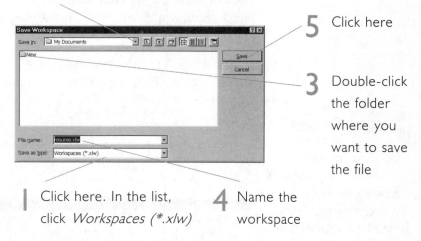

5 Click here

3 Double-click the folder where you want to save the file

1 Click here. In the list, click *Workspaces (*.xlw)*

4 Name the workspace

Opening a workspace

Pull down the File menu and click Open. Now follow steps 1-2 on page 49, but choose Workspaces (*.xlw) in the drop-down list. Finally, follow steps 3-6.

Closing workbooks

Closing one workbook

To close the active workbook, pull down the File menu and click Close.

If you've made amendments to the workbook but haven't yet saved them, Excel now launches a special message. Do the following:

| Click here to save your work
then close the workbook

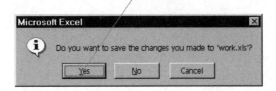

Closing all open workbooks

Hold down one Shift key. Pull down the File menu and click Close All.

If you've made amendments to any of the workbooks but haven't yet saved them, Excel launches a special message. Carry out either step 1 OR 2 below, as appropriate:

Re step 1 – if other open workbooks have unsaved amendments, Excel launches additional versions of this message; complete them as appropriate.

| Click here to save your work in
(then close) the first workbook

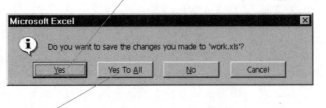

2 Click here to save your work in
(then close) *all* open workbooks

Cell referencing

In this chapter, you'll learn how to define cell references. You'll apply relative and absolute references, then discover how to use an older but easier-to-use system: R1C1 referencing. Next, you'll apply names to cells (a technique which makes cell manipulation much more convenient) and delete existing names. Finally, you'll have Excel replace references in formulas with their equivalent names, and paste names into formulas.

Covers

Chapter Five

Relative references

Excel lets you define cell references in various ways. Look at the next illustration:

	A	B	C	D	E
1					
2		Product	Unit Price	Quantity	Amount due
3		Widgets	£0.07	425	£29.75
4		Nuts	£0.13	246	
5		Bolts	£0.08	380	

The following formula has been inserted in cell E3:

C3*D3

This tells Excel to multiply the contents of C3 by D3. C3 and D3 are defined in relation to E3: C3 is in the same row (3) but two columns to the left (C), while D3 is in the same row but *one* column to the left. Excel calls this 'relative referencing'.

That these are relative references can be shown in the following way. If we use the techniques discussed on page 30 (AutoFill) to extend the formula in E3 to E4 and E5, this is the result:

HANDY TIP

The formulas in E3:E5 **have been made visible by pressing Ctrl+'.** **To hide the formulas again, repeat this.**

	C	D	E
1			
2	Unit Price	Quantity	Amount due
3	0.07	425	=C3*D3
4	0.13	246	=C4*D4
5	0.08	380	=C5*D5

Extrapolated cell references

Excel has extrapolated the references intelligently, correctly divining that the formula in E4 should be C4*D4, and that in E5 C5*D5.

Compare this process with the use of absolute (i.e. unchanging) references on page 55.

Absolute references

We've seen – on page 54 – how useful relative cell references can be. However, there are situations when you need to refer to one or more cells in a way which *doesn't* vary according to circumstances.

Look at the next illustration:

	A	B	C	D	E	F
1	VAT rate=	17.50%				
2		**Product**	**Unit Price**	**Quantity**	**Amount due**	**VAT**
3		Widgets	£0.07	425	£29.75	£5.21
4		Nuts	£0.13	246	£31.98	
5		Bolts	£0.08	380	£30.40	

HANDY TIP **The reason the VAT rate is entered separately from the calculation is convenience: if the rate changes, it's much easier to update one entry, rather than several.**

Cell F3 contains a formula which multiplies E3 by B1. If this were inserted as:

=E3*B1

extrapolating the formula over F4 and F5 (with the technique we used on page 54) would produce =E4*B2 and =E5*B3 respectively.

Clearly, this is incorrect (in this instance) because the cell in which the VAT rate is entered doesn't vary. It's an absolute reference, and remains B1.

Entering absolute references

Entering an absolute reference is easy. Simply insert $ in front of each formula component which won't change.

HANDY TIP **You can also use mixed cell references – i.e. combinations of relative and absolute references.**

The correct version of the VAT formula in F3 would therefore be:

=E3*B1

R1C1 referencing

Excel can also make use of an older, alternative style of referencing cells (called the 'R1C1' method) by which both columns and rows are numbered. It has the advantage that the distinction between absolute and relative referencing is easier to understand. Its disadvantage is that it is not as brief as the A1 method (Excel's default).

Relative and absolute R1C1 referencing

In R1C1 style, Excel indicates absolute references as per the following example:

R2C2   the equivalent of B2 in A1 style

In other words, cell location is defined with an 'R' followed by a row number and a 'C' followed by a column number.

On the other hand, R1C1 relative references are enclosed in square brackets. Thus, if the active cell is B5, the relative cell reference R[1]C[1] refers to the cell one row down and one column to the right, or C6.

Implementing R1C1 referencing

Pull down the Tools menu and click Options. Now do the following:

Activate this tab

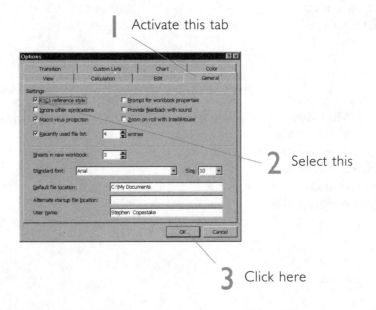

2 Select this

3 Click here

Naming cells (1)

An alternative way to reference cells is to give them a 'name' or identifier which describes the contents. Naming cells is a much more user-friendly technique than working with cell coordinates.

Defining names with the Name box

The easiest way to define names for cells is to use the Name box on the Formula Bar. Select the cell(s) you want to name, then do the following:

Names (it doesn't matter if they're lower or upper case) may be up to 255 characters long. The following rules apply:

- **The first character must be a letter or underscore (_).**
- **Other characters may be any sequence of letters and digits** *(but not spaces).*
- **Separators (as in the example on the right) must be either an underscore or full stop.**

Click here

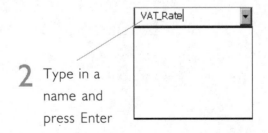

2 Type in a name and press Enter

Naming cells (2)

The Name box is an effective shortcut to applying and inserting names. However, you can also use a more comprehensive menu route to:

- define and apply new names

- apply existing names

- delete names

- substitute already defined names for cell references, either in selected cells or globally

- paste names into the Formula Bar

Defining/applying names – the menu route

Select the cell(s) to be named. Pull down the Insert menu and do the following:

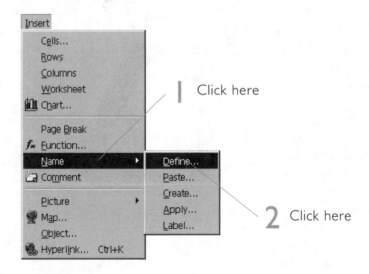

Carry out the additional steps on page 59.

Naming cells (3)

Now carry out step 1 OR 2 below. Finally, perform step 3:

Type in a new name

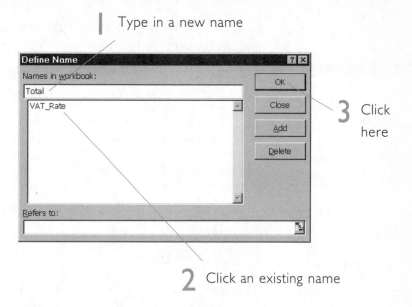

3 Click here

2 Click an existing name

Deleting names

Pull down the Insert menu and click Name, Define. Carry out the following steps:

Click a name

3 Click here

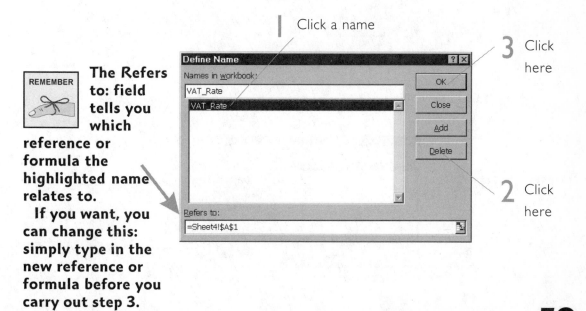

REMEMBER

The Refers to: field tells you which reference or formula the highlighted name relates to.
 If you want, you can change this: simply type in the new reference or formula before you carry out step 3.

2 Click here

Naming cells (4)

You can have Excel automatically replace normal cell references in formulas with the appropriate names.

Substituting names for references

Do ONE of the following:

1. Select the cells which contain the formulas whose references you want converted to the relevant names

2. Click any one cell in the worksheet if you want *all* formula references converted to the relevant names

Then pull down the Insert menu and carry out the following steps:

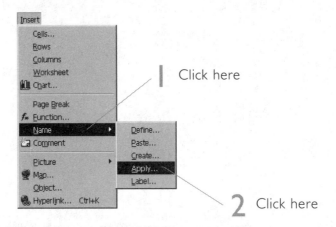

Click here

2 Click here

3 Click a name

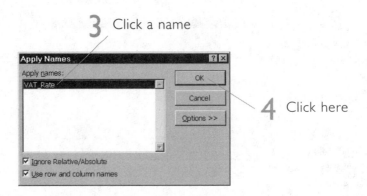

4 Click here

Naming cells (5)

Excel lets you paste names directly into the Formula Bar while you're entering a formula.

Pasting names
Activate the Formula Bar by clicking it. Begin the formula by typing:

=

Now pull down the Insert menu and do the following:

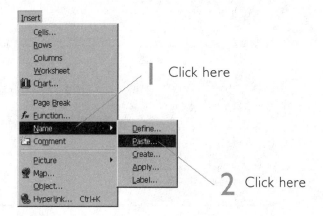

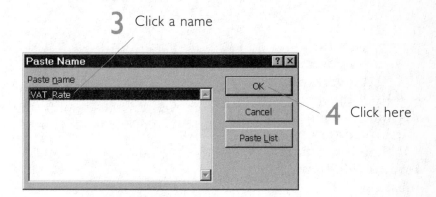

Cell reference operators

We've already encountered one cell reference operator: the colon. This is known as the Range operator and is used to define the rectangular block of cells formed between the two cell references which it separates. For example:

A5:E7

defines the block of cells which begins with A5 and ends with E7.

However, there are two other reference operators. Look at the next illustration:

	A	B	C	D	E
1					
2		Qtr1	Qtr2	Qtr3	Qtr4
3	**1996**	8000	10000	15000	12000
4	**1997**	9000	11000	17000	13000
5	**1998**	10000	12000	19000	14000
6					
7	Quarter 3 sales for 1996-1998=				51000
8	Quarter 3 sales for 1997=				17000

E7 contains this formula:

=SUM(D3,D4,D5)

The comma is known as the Union operator; it combines multiple references into one. In this case, the formula is totalling separate cells which could also be expressed as: D3:D5. However, this need not be the case. For instance, it could show: A3,B5,E8...

E8 contains the following formula:

=SUM(B4:E4 D3:D5)

The space separating the two ranges is known as the Intersection operator. The formula returns the cell at the intersection of B4:E4 and D3:D5 – in other words, D4.

Functions

In this chapter, you'll learn how to insert functions into your formulas. Excel has a very large number of inbuilt functions which perform specialised calculations for wide-ranging applications e.g. statistical, mathematical, financial, etc. You'll learn how to utilise some of the most frequently used functions. You'll also discover how to use the simpler functions on-the-fly, by reference to Excel's Status bar.

Chapter Six

Covers

Functions – an overview

Functions are pre-defined tools which accomplish specific tasks. These tasks are often calculations; occasionally, however, they're more generalised (e.g. some functions simply return dates and/or times). In effect, functions replace one or more formulas.

Excel provides a special dialog – the Formula Palette – to help ensure that you enter functions correctly. This is useful for the following reasons:

- Excel provides so many functions, it's very convenient to apply (and amend) them from a centralised source

- the Formula Palette ensures the functions are entered with the correct syntax

Functions can only be used in formulas.

Recognising functions

Functions are always followed by open and closed brackets. The following are often-used examples:

SUM	Adds together a range of numbers
AVERAGE	Finds the average of a range of numbers
MAX	Finds the largest number in a range
MIN	Finds the smallest number in a range
LOOKUP	Compares a specified value with a specified cell range and returns a value
IF	Verifies if a condition is true or false, and acts accordingly

Some of these functions are explored further in the course of this chapter.

Inserting a function

HANDY TIP

You can also use another route to insert a function. Click in a cell. Pull down the Insert menu and click Function. In the Function category field in the Paste Function dialog, select a heading. Click a function in the Function name box. Click OK. Excel now launches the Formula Palette – complete steps 4 and 5.

Inserting a function with the Formula Palette

At the relevant juncture during the process of inserting a formula, refer to the Formula Bar and do the following:

Click here

Now carry out the following steps:

2 Click here

HANDY TIP

To edit an existing function, click the relevant cell. Click this button:

in the Formula Bar. The Formula Palette launches, with the first function displayed. Amend this (or a later) function and/or its arguments. Click OK when you've finished.

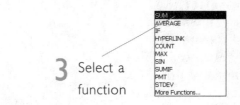

3 Select a function

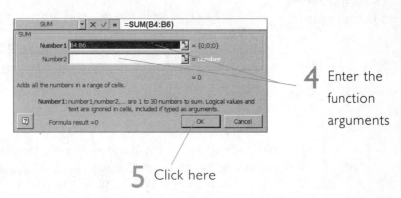

4 Enter the function arguments

5 Click here

The SUM function

The SUM function can be used to automatically total adjacent cells. You can insert a SUM function by using the Formula Palette – see page 65. However, you can also use a useful shortcut: AutoSum. Look at the next illustration:

	A	B	C	D	E	F
1						
2		Qtr1	Qtr2	Qtr3	Qtr4	Totals
3	1996	8000	10000	15000	12000	
4	1997	9000	11000	17000	13000	
5	1998	10000	12000	19000	14000	

To total the range B3:E3 in F3, click F3. Now do the following:

Click here

Excel surrounds the cells it believes should be included in the SUM function with a dotted line:

	A	B	C	D	E	F
1						
2		Qtr1	Qtr2	Qtr3	Qtr4	Totals
3	1996	8000	10000	15000	12000	=SUM(A3:E3)
4	1997	9000	11000	17000	13000	
5	1998	10000	12000	19000	14000	
6	Totals					

Amend the formula entry in F3, if necessary (in this instance, change A3:E3 to B3:E3). Then press Enter; Excel inserts the SUM function.

HANDY TIP

You can use a shortcut here. Pre-select the cells you want to total *before* you carry out step 1. For instance, if you select B3:F6 and then click the AutoSum button, this is the result:

		Qtr1	Qtr2	Qtr3	Qtr4	Totals
3	1996	8000	10000	15000	12000	45000
4	1997	9000	11000	17000	13000	50000
5	1998	10000	12000	19000	14000	55000
6	Totals	27000	33000	51000	39000	150000

Excel has inserted *all* relevant totals

The LOOKUP function (1)

There are two forms of the LOOKUP function:
• **Vector**
• **Array**
Here, we're using the Array version.

LOOKUP compares a value you set (the Look-Up value) with the first row or column in a Look-Up table. If it finds a matching value, it returns it in the cell you specify. If it doesn't, it returns the largest value in the table which is the same as or less than the Look-Up value

Alternatively, if the Look-Up value is smaller than all the values in the Look-Up table, LOOKUP returns the following error:

#N/A

Study the next illustration:

LOOKUP can also work with text values and/or names.

Look-Up value

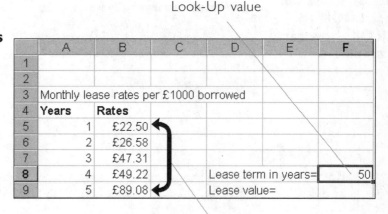

	A	B	C	D	E	F
1						
2						
3	Monthly lease rates per £1000 borrowed					
4	Years	Rates				
5	1	£22.50				
6	2	£26.58				
7	3	£47.31				
8	4	£49.22		Lease term in years=		50
9	5	£89.08		Lease value=		

Look-Up table

The values in the Look-Up table must be in ascending order.
   If they're not, you can rectify this. Select the values. Pull down the Data menu and click Sort. If the Sort Warning dialog appears, click Sort. In the Sort by field in the Sort dialog, make sure Ascending is selected. Finally, click OK.

Here, a Look-Up table and value have been established. (In this instance, names have also been applied: the table is Lease_Table, while the value is Lease_Term.)

It only remains to enter and define the LOOKUP function – see page 68 for how to do this.

The LOOKUP function (2)

Using LOOKUP

Select the relevant cell (in the example on page 67, F9).
Follow steps 1-2 on page 65. Now carry out the following
steps:

Select the relevant cell (in the example on page 67, F9).
Follow steps 1-2 on page 65.

HANDY TIP

**Re step 1 –
if
LOOKUP
isn't listed,**
click More
Functions instead.
   In the Function
category field in the
Paste Function
dialog, click Lookup
& Reference. In the
Function name box,
select LOOKUP.
Click OK. Now carry
out steps 2-6.

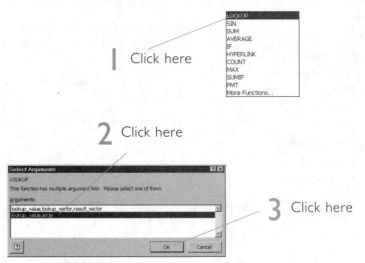

| Click here

2 Click here

3 Click here

4 Type in the Look-Up value reference

REMEMBER

**Re steps 4
and 5 –
here,
names**
have been used for
convenience.

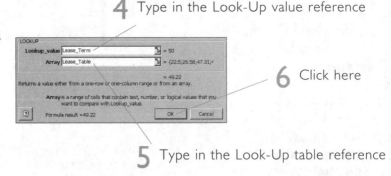

6 Click here

5 Type in the Look-Up table reference

The final result:
LOOKUP has
returned the highest
value under 50

The IF function (1)

The IF function checks whether a specified condition is TRUE or FALSE and carries out one or more specified actions accordingly.

Look at the next illustration:

	A	B	C	D
1				
2				
3		Name	Amount Spent	Discount
4				
5		Brierley	1,280	
6		Jones	1,020	
7		Mitchell	570	
8		Harrison	1150	
9		Wood	870	

Individual customer discounts need to be calculated in D5:D9

Each discount in D5:D9 depends on the following conditions:

* if the amount a customer has spent is greater than or equal to £1000, then the discount is 20%

* if the amount a customer spent is less than £1000 then the discount is 10%

Using the IF Function

First, select the cell you want to host the function – in this case, D5 (initially). Follow steps 1-2 on page 65. Now carry out step 1 below:

HANDY TIP

Re step 1 – if IF isn't listed, click More Functions instead. In the Function category field in the Paste Function dialog, click Logical. In the Function name box, select IF. Click OK.

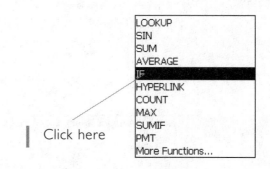

Click here

Perform the remaining steps on page 70.

The IF function (2)

Carry out the following additional steps:

Enter the 'logical test'

HANDY TIP

See the Glossary below for an explanation of the terms used in this dialog.

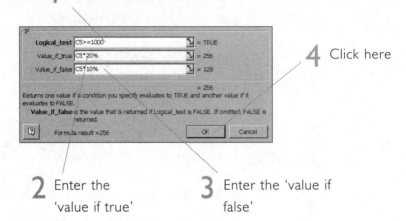

4 Click here

2 Enter the 'value if true'

3 Enter the 'value if false'

REMEMBER

The IF function uses comparison operators – see page 33 for details.

Glossary

Logical test — The condition. In this instance: C5>=1000 (i.e. the contents of C5 must be greater than or equal to 1000)

Value if true — The action to be taken if the condition is met. In this instance: C5*20% (i.e. the contents of C5 are multiplied by 20%)

Value if false — The action to be taken if the condition isn't met. In this instance: C5*10% (i.e. the contents of C5 are multiplied by 10%)

Name	Amount Spent	Discount
Brierley	1,280	256
Jones	1,020	204
Mitchell	570	57
Harrison	1150	230
Wood	870	87

The IF function has been inserted into D5, and extrapolated into D6:D9 with AutoFill

Cell errors and auditing

This chapter provides details of common error messages which arise when Excel is unable to evaluate a formula. These are shown 'on-the-fly', with reference to specific examples and also with the appropriate corrections. Excel supplies a set of auditing tools to help trace errors. You'll learn how to use these to track dependent and precedent cells. You'll also use the Error Tracer to pinpoint cells which are in conflict with formulas. Finally, you'll insert comments into cells, and edit them subsequently.

Covers

Chapter Seven

Cell errors (1)

The following table shows details of some of the common Excel error messages (they're shown in action in the illustration below).

#DIV/0!	This error is caused by an attempt to divide 2.5 by zero. Theoretically this should generate infinity. In practice any such value is too big, even for a computer, and the calculation is suppressed
#N/A	This means that No value is Available. The LOOKUP argument (B8, B5:D6) should refer to cell D8; B8 – since it contains text – is incorrect.
#NAME?	Excel fails to recognise the Name of the function 'IS', which has been incorrectly typed for 'IF'
#NULL!	This formula uses the intersection operator (a space) to locate the cell at the intersection of ranges B15:D15 and A16:A18. Since they don't intersect, Excel displays the error message

The data/ error messages are on the left of the illustration; the formulas which gave rise to the errors are on the right.

	A	B	C	D	D
1	(1)				
2		2.5	0	#DIV/0!	=B2/C2
3					
4	(2)				
5	Amount:	£0	£500	£1,000	1000
6	Discount:	0.0%	5.0%	10.0%	0.1
7					
8		Price =		£750	750
9		Discount Rate =		#N/A	=LOOKUP(B8, B5:D6)
10					
11	(3)				
12		·-0.25		#NAME?	=IS(B12=0, "Zero", "Non-zero")
13					
14	(4)				
15		5	10	15	15
16	2				
17	4				
18	6			#NULL!	=B15:D15 A16:A18

The above error messages in action

Cell errors (2)

Here are some additional error messages, and details of their causes:

#NUM! This error value indicates problems with numbers. The first example of this error (see below) attempts to generate the value 100^{1000}, i.e. 100 multiplied by itself 1000 times, which is too large for the computer to store and the calculation is suppressed. ·

In the second example the attempt to calculate the square root (SQRT function) of a negative value is suppressed.

#VALUE! This error occurs when the data in a cell isn't appropriate for the operation, or the operation doesn't apply to the type of data. Here an attempt has been made to divide 'Text' by 50.

This error is not necessarily generated by a formula. In this case the number stored is simply too long for the cell width.

REMEMBER

The data/ error messages are on the left of the illustration; the formulas which gave rise to the errors are on the right.

A20	↓		'(5)		
	A	**B**	**C**	**D**	**D**
20	(5)				
21		100	1000	#NUM!	=B21^C21
22		16		#NUM!	=SQRT(-B22)
23					
24	(6)				
25		Text	50	#VALUE!	=B25/C25
26					
27	(7)				
28				########	100000000
29					
30	(8)				
31		100			
32			50	2	=B31/C32

Cell errors (3)

REMEMBER

The examples on pages 72-74 are simple, practical illustrations of the causes of error messages. In practice, tracking down the origin of an error message is sometimes less than straightforward, because a single error may cause a proliferation of error values.
   (See pages 75-77 for tracking techniques.)

The final error message we'll discuss here is slightly more complex:

#REF!   To generate this error requires another
                     stage. On page 73, the final formula
                     =B31/C32
                     divides the contents of cell B31 by the
                     contents of cell C32, initially producing the
                     correct answer. However, if Excel can't
                     locate one of the cells referred to (for
                     instance, if B31 no longer exists because
                     row 31 has been deleted), it displays this
                     message.

This process is demonstrated in the illustration below:

B The formula has changed; the B31
   component has been replaced by
   #REF! and C32 has now become C31

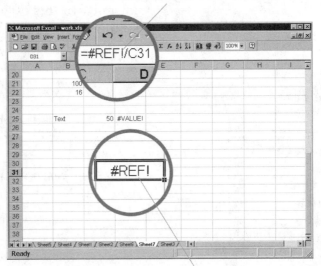

A Since row 31 has been deleted and the
   reference in the formula to B31 is invalid,
   Excel displays the error message

HANDY TIP

#REF! only appears if you've *deleted* the cell referred to by a formula; clearing the cell's contents (by selecting it and clicking Clear, Contents in the Edit menu) will, instead, produce: 0.

Auditing tools (1)

Auditing displays tracer arrows between cells. In order to make these arrows more visible, you may wish to hide worksheet gridlines.
Pull down the Tools menu and click Options. Activate the View tab; in the Window options section, select Gridlines. Finally, click OK.

Excel provides a variety of features you can use to ensure formulas work correctly. You can use the Auditing toolbar to have Excel delineate cell relationships with arrows ('tracers'). In this way, if a formula returns an error message, you can track down which cell is misbehaving.

Cells which are referred to by a formula in another cell are called precedents. For example, if cell H26 has the formula:

=J97

J97 is a precedent.

Inserting precedent tracers

Click the cell whose precedents you want to display. Pull down the Tools menu and click Auditing, Show Auditing Toolbar. Now do the following:

Click here

Before carrying out the procedures here, pull down the Tools menu and click Options. Activate the View tab; in the Objects section, ensure 'Show all' is selected. Finally, click OK.

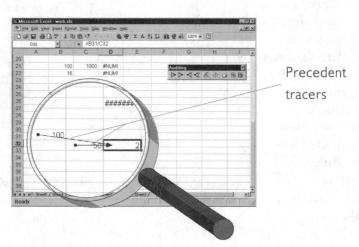

Precedent tracers

Auditing tools (2)

Cells which contain formulas referring to other cells are called dependents. For instance, if cell H6 has the formula:

=SUM(C6:D8)

HANDY TIP

To remove all tracer arrows on the worksheet (e.g. when you've finished the audit, or perhaps to start again from a different cell), simply click this button:

H6 is a dependent cell (and the cells in the range C6:D8 are precedent cells – see page 75).

Inserting dependent tracers

Select a cell which is referred to in a formula. Pull down the Tools menu and click Auditing, Show Auditing Toolbar. Now do the following:

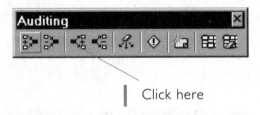

in the Auditing toolbar.

Click here

BEWARE

Before carrying out the procedures here, pull down the Tools menu and click Options. Activate the View tab; in the Objects section, ensure 'Show all' is selected. Finally, click OK.

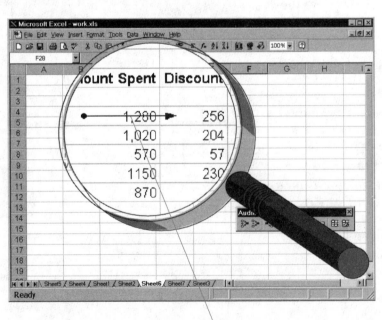

Dependent tracer

Using the Error Tracer

 The Error Tracer locates all cells affected by the original error.

When a formula returns an error, you can use another auditing tool – the Error Tracer – to track it back to its source and then correct it.

Using the Error Tracer

Select a cell which contains an error value. Pull down the Tools menu and click Auditing, Show Auditing Toolbar. Now do the following:

 Before carrying out the procedures here, pull down the Tools menu and click Options. Activate the View tab; in the Objects section, ensure 'Show all' is selected. Finally, click OK.

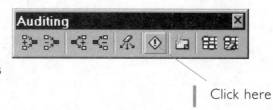

Click here

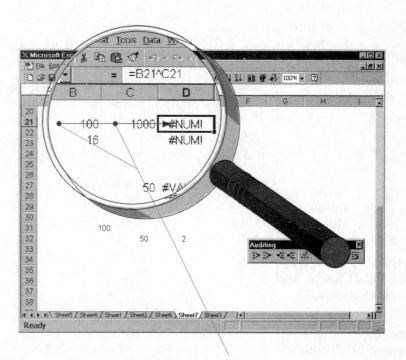

 Always clear existing tracer arrows by clicking this button in the Auditing toolbar:

before reusing the Error Tracer.

Excel flags all cells referred to by the incorrect formula

Working with comments

You can attach comments to cells. Once inserted, comments can be viewed or edited at will.

Inserting a comment

Select the relevant cell. Pull down the Insert menu and click Comment. Now do the following:

To view a comment (without editing it), simply move the mouse pointer over the relevant cell.

Comment box

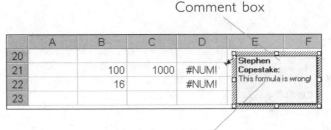

Type in the comment, then click outside the box

Cells which contain a comment have the following:

Comment flag

Editing a comment

Select the relevant cell (for how to recognise cells which contain comments, see the Remember tip). Pull down the Insert menu and click Edit Comment. Now click inside the Comment box and amend the text as necessary. Click outside the box when you've finished.

Deleting a comment

Click any cell which contains a comment. Pull down the Insert menu and click Edit Comment. Now do the following:

If the Comment flag *doesn't* **appear, pull down the Tools menu and click Options. Activate the View tab. Select Comment indicator only or Comment & indicator. Click OK.**

Click the Comment box frame, then press Delete

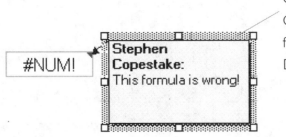

Workbook security

In this chapter, you'll restrict access to your workbooks by allocating passwords, then reopen them. You'll also prevent unauthorised users from modifying the structure of constituent worksheets and resizing workbook windows. Finally, you'll 'protect' worksheets, a technique which allows you to specify precisely which cells can and can't be amended.

Covers

Chapter Eight

Protecting workbooks (1)

REMEMBER

Passwords are case-sensitive, and can be up to 15 characters long. They can be any combination of letters, digits and other symbols.

You can protect your workbooks by:

- allocating an 'Open' password

- allocating a 'Modify' password

The first allows users to open the associated workbook but prevents them from saving changes *under the existing filename*. The second, on the other hand, allows users to modify and save the workbook.

You impose passwords in the course of carrying out a Save As operation

BEWARE

If you lose or forget the password, the file cannot be recovered.

Allocating a password

Pull down the File menu and click Save As. Carry out steps 1-4 on page 45, then click the Options button. Now perform steps 1 and/or 2 below, as appropriate. Finally, carry out step 3:

HANDY TIP

After step 3, Excel launches a verifying dialog. Do the following:

B Click here

A Retype your password

Note: if you carried out steps 1 AND 2, two dialogs launch. Complete both.

1 Type in an Open password

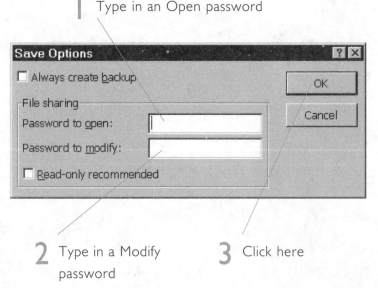

2 Type in a Modify password

3 Click here

Finally, carry out step 5 on page 45 to save the workbook with its password(s).

Protecting workbooks (2)

Opening a password-protected file
Follow steps 1-6 on page 49. Now do the following:

Once passwords have been allocated to a file, you can modify or remove them.

With the file open, pull down the File menu and click Save As. Carry out steps 1-4 on page 45. Click the Options button. Now do the following:

Type in the password

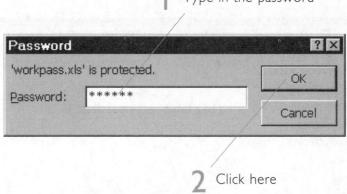

2 Click here

If the workbook you're opening has had both Open and Modify passwords allocated to it, Excel launches a further dialog. Carry out steps 1 and 2 below to open the workbook with the ability to modify it and save changes under the original name. Alternatively, carry out step 3 to open the workbook as a 'read-only' file (i.e. any amendments you make subsequently must be saved under a different name).

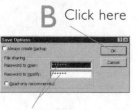

B Click here

A Retype or delete the passwords

If you amended 1 or 2 passwords in step A, Excel launches the Confirm Password dialog; complete this as per steps A and ß on page 80.

Type in the second password

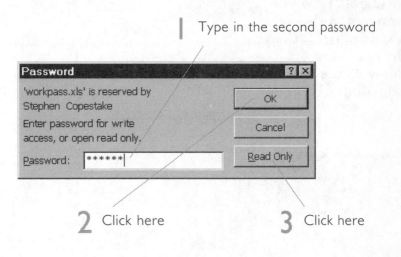

2 Click here   3 Click here

Protecting workbook structure

You can 'protect' the following workbook aspects:

- structure (this prevents worksheets from being deleted, renamed, moved or inserted)

- windows (this prevents workbook windows from being resized, moved or closed)

As a result of the above, certain menu commands are greyed out.

Protecting a workbook

Pull down the Tools menu and do the following:

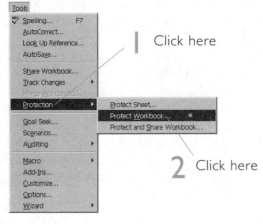

Click here

2 Click here

   Now do the following:

3 Click either or both of these

B Click here

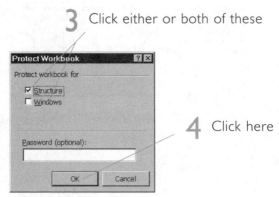

4 Click here

A Retype your password

Protecting worksheets (1)

You can have Excel warn you when you're about to open a workbook containing macros (small, independent programs – see Chapter 14) which *might* contain harmful viruses.
   Pull down the Tools menu and click Options. Activate the General tab and ensure 'Macro virus protection' is ticked.
   Note that Excel can't actually verify whether viruses are present; it can only warn you of the possibility...

Cells can be protected so that their contents are not overwritten. This is a two-stage process:

1. 'Unlocking' those cells which you'll want to amend *after* the host worksheet has been protected (you won't be able to modify any of the other cells)

2. Protecting the worksheet

Unlocking cells

Select the cells you want to unlock. Pull down the Format menu and do the following:

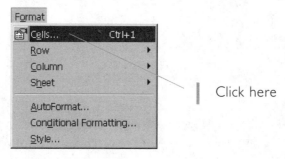

Click here

2 Ensure this tab is activated

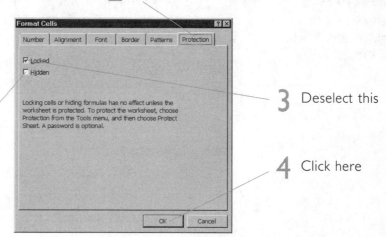

If you select this field, the formula(s) in the selected cell(s) will be hidden.

3 Deselect this

4 Click here

Protecting worksheets (2)

Protecting the host worksheet
Pull down the Format menu and do the following:

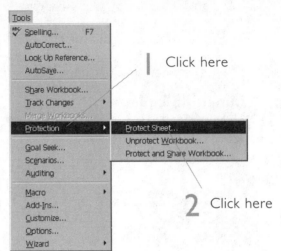

Click here

2 Click here

HANDY TIP If you want to modify cell protection, pull down the Tools menu and click Unprotect Sheet. Then select the relevant cells. Pull down the Format menu and click Cells. Activate the Protection tab in the Format Cells dialog; select or deselect Locked, as appropriate. Finally, click OK.

The effects of cell protection
When you've protected cells, the following results apply:

1. Any attempt to overwrite/edit a locked cell produces a special message:

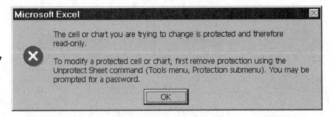

2. When a locked cell is selected, certain menu commands are greyed out

3. If a locked cell is selected, pressing Tab will move the cursor to the next locked cell (the movement is from top to bottom, and left to right). Pressing Shift+Tab reverses the direction.

Data analysis

In this chapter, you'll explore how to preview changes to selected data values and gauge the effect on the overall data pattern, and how to extrapolate predictions based on current figures and formulas. You'll also switch to manual (rather than automatic) calculation, a useful technique in especially large worksheets.

Covers

Chapter Nine

Data analysis – an overview

Look at the following worksheet extract:

	A	B	C	D
1				
2		Video Rentals		
3				
4		Rental Price=		£2.00
5		Number of Rentals=		250
6		Total Income=		£500
7				
8		Total Costs=		£200
9				
10		Net Profit=		£300
11				

Here, we have a simple worksheet which calculates the Net Profit based on several data values relating to the renting out of videos.

You should bear the following in mind:

Total Income (D6) = Rental Price (D4) x Number of Rentals (D5)

Net Profit (D10)   = Total Income (D6) – Total Costs (D8)

See the Handy Tip for details of formulas contained in the extract.

Later topics in this chapter will explore various techniques which allow you to interpolate data into the extract conveniently and easily. Once interpolated, changes to data values will ripple through the extract automatically, and can be viewed (and later discarded, if required) at will.

Automatic v. manual calculation

By default, Excel automatically recalculates formulas in dependent cells when the values in precedent cells are changed. Usually this occurs so rapidly there is no noticeable delay. However, if the network of dependent formulas is especially large and complex you may well have to wait for the update to finish. This can prove particularly frustrating if you wish to change several values and are made to wait after each one while the rest of the worksheet is recalculated.

You can, though, if you want, opt to have formulas calculated manually, as often or as infrequently as you wish.

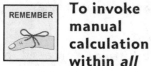

To invoke manual calculation within *all* open worksheets, simply press F9.

Turning on manual calculation

Pull down the Tools menu and click Options. Now do the following:

To invoke manual calculation within the active worksheet only, press Shift+F9.

Activate this tab

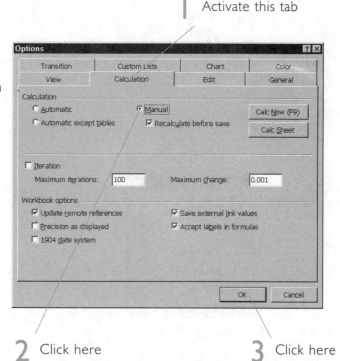

2 Click here

3 Click here

Using Goal Seek (1)

Please refer back to the illustration on page 86 and consider the following:

Let's suppose we need to know the number of video rentals necessary to break even. In other words, we want to find out how many rentals are necessary to meet the total costs, thereby ensuring that the net profit is £0. In the case of a simple example like this, you could arrive at the correct figure manually, by trial and error, without too much time and effort. However, more complex worksheets would clearly make this approach impracticable.

Instead, however, you can use a Goal Seek What-If test.

Applying a Goal Seek What-If test

First, select the cell which contains the formula you need to resolve (in this instance, D10). Pull down the Tools menu and do the following:

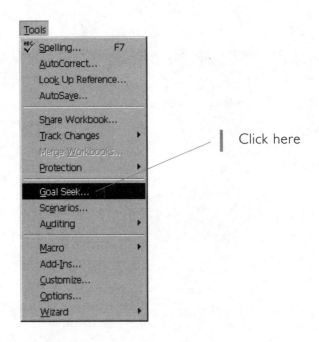

Click here

Using Goal Seek (2)

Now carry out the following steps:

2 Type in the target value (in this case, '0')

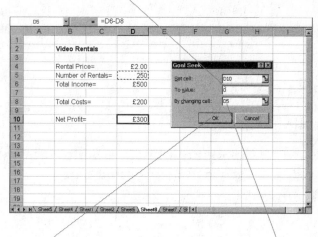

4 Click here

3 Type in the reference of the cell you want to change (in this case, D5)

Excel has calculated the What-If value…

HANDY TIP

Re step 5 – click the Cancel button instead if you don't want the result of the Goal Seek inserted into your worksheet.

The ability not to implement the Goal Seek results makes this a useful technique for exploring alternatives.

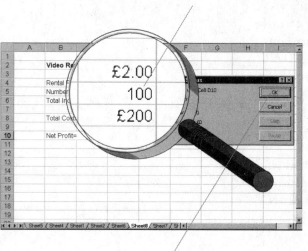

5 Click here to update the worksheet

One-variable data tables (1)

Please refer back to the illustration on page 86 and consider the following additional hypothesis:

Let's suppose we wanted to know how the Net Profit would change when the Rental Price is changed. We could do this using the simple What-If technique of varying the Rental Price and recording the corresponding change in the Net Profit. However, it would be necessary to repeat this for as many separate rental price values as we wished to test.

A much simpler and quicker route is to use a one-variable data table.

Applying a one-variable data table

Carry out the following steps:

Re step 2 – enter the formula which returns the Net Profit. Here, you simply refer to the relevant cell: =D10

Re step 2 – if you insert values in a column, the formula cell must be in the row above the first value, and one cell to the right. If you type in values in a row, however, it must be in the column to the left of the first value, and one cell below. One-variable tables will only work if these conditions are met.

2 Type in the necessary formula (but see the tips on the left)

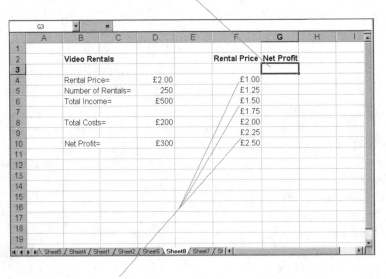

In a row or column, type in the values for which you want to generate alternatives

	A	B	C	D	E	F	G	H	I
1									
2		Video Rentals				Rental Price	Net Profit		
3									
4		Rental Price=		£2.00		£1.00			
5		Number of Rentals=		250		£1.25			
6		Total Income=		£500		£1.50			
7						£1.75			
8		Total Costs=		£200		£2.00			
9						£2.25			
10		Net Profit=		£300		£2.50			

One-variable data tables (2)

Now select the table. Pull down the Data menu and click Table. Then carry out the following steps:

You must select *both* columns or rows (but not the headings).

The selected table

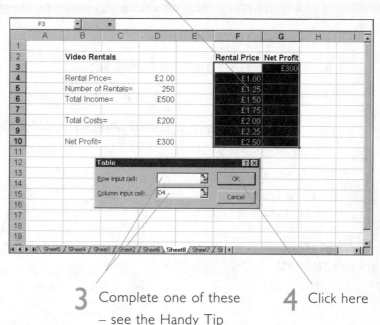

Re step 3 – complete the Column input cell field if you created a columnar table, the Row input cell field if you created a row-based table.
You should enter the reference of the input cell for which the initial table values (in this case, F4:F10) are to be substituted. Here, enter: D4.

3 Complete one of these – see the Handy Tip

4 Click here

Rental Price	Net Profit
	£300
£1.00	50
£1.25	112.5
£1.50	175
£1.75	237.5
£2.00	300
£2.25	362.5
£2.50	425

The completed one-variable table

Two-variable data tables (1)

Please refer back to the illustration on page 86 and consider the following:

So far, the examples we've examined have been fairly simple. Suppose, however, that we need to know how the Net Profit would vary relative to *both* of the following:

- the Rental Price

- the Number of Rentals

For this, we need to use a two-variable data table.

Applying a two-variable data table
Refer to the illustration below and do the following:

Re step 1 – the correct cell reference in this example is: F4.

| Select the cell at the intersection of the row containing the first input values and the column containing the second

	D	E	F	G	H	I	J	K
1								
2			Rental			Net Profit		
3			Price		Number of Rentals			
4	£2.00		£300.00	100	125	150	175	200
5	250		£1.00					
6	£500		£1.25					
7			£1.50					
8	£200		£1.75					
9			£2.00					
10	£300		£2.25					
11			£2.50					

Re step 2 – in this example, the input categories are:
- **rental price**
- **number of rentals**
Therefore, the cell which relates to them is D10 (i.e. Net Profit) and the formula is:

=D10

2 Type in the formula which relates to the two input categories

Two-variable data tables (2)

Now select the table. This stage is crucial. The selection must include:

- the formula cell (F4 in the example on page 92)

- the row and column of input data (F5:F11,G4:K4 in the example on page 92)

- the empty body of the table (G5:K11 in the example on page 92)

Pull down the Data menu and click Table; do the following:

Re step 3 - **in the** **current** **example,** the cell which relates to the number of rentals is D5.

Re step 4 - **in the** **current** **example,** the cell which relates to the rental price is D4.

3 Type in the reference for the cell which relates to the number of rentals

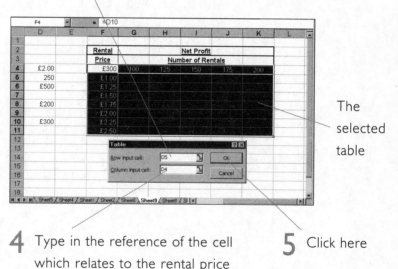

The selected table

4 Type in the reference of the cell which relates to the rental price

5 Click here

The table **shows at a** **glance the** **rental** price/number of rentals relationship.

Rental Price	Net Profit Number of Rentals				
£300	100	125	150	175	200
£1.00	-£100.00	-£75.00	-£50.00	-£25.00	£0.00
£1.25	-£75.00	-£43.75	-£12.50	£18.75	£50.00
£1.50	-£50.00	-£12.50	£25.00	£62.50	£100.00
£1.75	-£25.00	£18.75	£62.50	£106.25	£150.00
£2.00	£0.00	£50.00	£100.00	£150.00	£200.00
£2.25	£25.00	£81.25	£137.50	£193.75	£250.00
£2.50	£50.00	£112.50	£175.00	£237.50	£300.00

The completed table

What-If scenarios (1)

Please refer back to the illustration on page 86 and consider the following:

Let's suppose we need to forecast the effect of changing the following values:

- the Rental Price (D4)

- the Number of Rentals (D5)

- the Total Cost (D8)

We could simply input revised values directly into the worksheet and observe the effects. However, if the revisions are simply putative, or if we need to input the same revisions more than once (or in varying combinations), it makes more sense to use a scenario.

A scenario is simply a set of values you use to forecast the outcome of a worksheet model. You can:

- create new scenarios

- switch to and view existing scenarios

- return to the original worksheet values by invoking Undo

Creating a What-If scenario

Pull down the Tools menu and do the following:

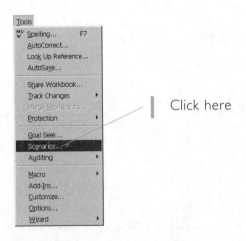

Click here

What-If scenarios (2)

Now carry out the following steps:

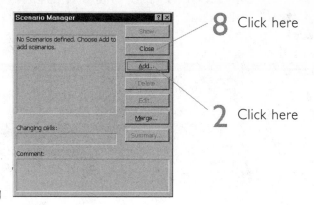

8 Click here

2 Click here

HANDY TIP

To amend values in an existing scenario, click this button:

in the Scenario Manager dialog. Now complete the Edit Scenario and Scenario Values dialogs in line with steps 3-7. Finally, perform step 8.

3 Name the scenario

5 Click here

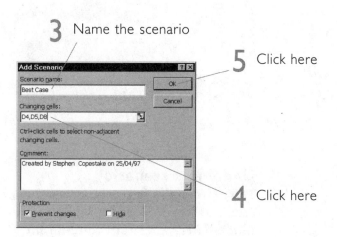

4 Click here

6 Type in What-if values

7 Click here

What-If scenarios (3)

Viewing a scenario

Pull down the Tools menu and click Scenario. Now do the following:

After step 2, Excel inserts the scenario values:

REMEMBER

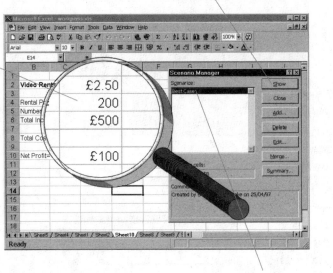

2 Click here

Click a scenario

Undoing a scenario

To revert to the data values which were in force before a scenario was imposed, pull down the Edit menu immediately afterwards and do the following:

Click here

Multiple worksheets/ workbooks

In this chapter, you'll learn how to create new worksheet windows and then rearrange them to best effect. You'll then set up data links between worksheets and workbooks, and create 3D references in formulas. Next, you'll discover how to achieve a useful overview by hiding rows and columns. Finally, you'll split worksheets into separate panes (so each can be viewed separately) and freeze them for independent scrolling.

Covers

Viewing several worksheets

Excel lets you view multiple worksheets simultaneously. This can be particularly useful when they have data in common. Viewing multiple worksheets is a two-stage process:

1.   opening a new window

2.   selecting the additional worksheet

Opening a new window
Pull down the Window menu and do the following:

HANDY TIP

To switch between active windows, pull down the Window menu and click the relevant entry in the list at the bottom.

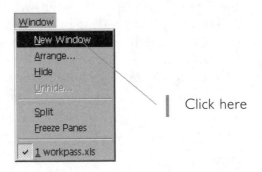

Click here

Selecting the additional worksheet
Excel now launches a new window showing an alternative view of the active worksheet. Do the following:

HANDY TIP

If you want to work with alternative views of the *same* worksheet – a useful technique in itself – simply omit step 2.

	A	B	C	D	E	F	G	H	I
1									
2		Video Rentals				Rental			Net Profit
3						Price			Number of Ren
4		Rental Price=		£2.50		£400	100	125	150
5		Number of Rentals=		200		£1.00	£0.00	£25.00	£50.00
6		Total Income=		£500		£1.25	£25.00	£56.25	£87.50
7						£1.50	£50.00	£87.50	£125.00
8		Total Costs=		£100		£1.75	£75.00	£118.75	£162.50
9						£2.00	£100.00	£150.00	£200.00
10		Net Profit=		£400		£2.25	£125.00	£181.25	£237.50
11						£2.50	£150.00	£212.50	£275.00
12									

2 Click the relevant sheet tab

Rearranging worksheet windows

When you have multiple worksheet windows open at once, you can have Excel arrange them in specific patterns. This is a useful technique because it makes worksheets more visible and accessible. The following options are available:

Tiled   Windows are displayed side by side:

Horizontal   Windows are displayed in a tiled column, with horizontal subdivisions:

Vertical   Windows are displayed in a tiled row, with vertical subdivisions:

Cascade   Windows are overlaid (with a slight offset):

Rearranging windows

Pull down the Window menu and click Arrange. Do the following:

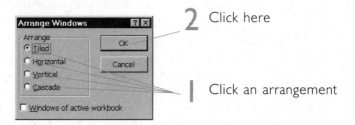

2 Click here

1 Click an arrangement

Links within a single workbook (1)

Consider the following examples:

	A	B	C	D	E
1		Sales Figures 1996			
2		Qtr1	Qtr2	Qtr3	Qtr4
3		£9,000.00	£11,000.00	£17,000.00	£13,000.00

	A	B	C	D	E
1		Sales Figures 1997			
2		Qtr1	Qtr2	Qtr3	Qtr4
3		£10,000.00	£12,000.00	£19,000.00	£14,000.00

You can also set up links between separate workbooks – see page 102.

Here, we have extracts from two separate worksheets within the same workbook. The first records sales figures for 1996, the second sales figures for 1997. In the excerpts shown, the amount of data is small; there is really no reason why both sets of data shouldn't have been recorded on a single worksheet. However, where you're concerned with large amounts of data, it's a very good idea to record them on separate worksheets. By the same token, if you needed to record the totals of both years it would be advantageous to use a third worksheet...

Using lots of smaller worksheets (as opposed to single, much larger sheets) produces the following benefits:

- your worksheets will recalculate faster (because large worksheets are much more unwieldy)

- it's much easier to remain in control of your worksheets

When you do use separate worksheets, you can 'link' the relevant data. To revert to the earlier example, the totals in the third worksheet could be linked to the relevant data in the 96 Sales and 97 Sales worksheets. If the contents of any of the relevant cells on these worksheets are changed, the totals are automatically updated.

Links within a single workbook (2)

Establishing links

Create the necessary additional worksheet. Then do the following:

Select the cell you want to link

This worksheet refers back to the illustrations on page 100.

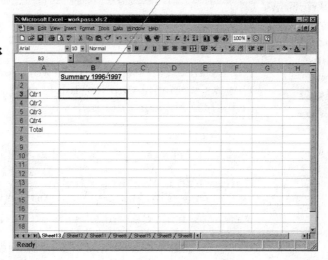

You can have cell references in formulas include worksheet names by separating the name and reference with '!' (but omit the quote marks).

For example, to refer to cell A18 in worksheet 12, type:

Sheet12!A18

within the formula.

Now type in the required formula. Follow these rules:

1. Type =

2. Type in the reference to the cell on the first worksheet

3. Type in the relevant operator: in this case, +

4. Type in the reference to the cell on the second worksheet

5. Press Enter

In our specific example (and given that the 1996 totals are on Sheet11 and the 97 totals on Sheet12), the formula will be:

=Sheet11!B3+Sheet12!B3

Links between workbooks

You can also insert links which relate to other workbooks, either open or on disk. Look at the illustration below:

	A	B
1		
2	1996	=SUM('C:\MY DOCUMENTS\[96_SALES.XLSSheet11]Sheet11'!B3)
3	1997	=SUM([97_SALES.XLS]Sheet12!B3)
4	1998	=Sheet2!B4
5		
6	Three Year Total	=SUM(B2:B4)

Space restrictions have forced the (apparent) line break in this formula; it isn't present within Excel.

This is an excerpt from a new workbook: 98_SALES.XLS. This, as its name implies, totals sales for the years 96-98 inclusive. The formula in B2 is:

=SUM('C:\MY DOCUMENTS\[96_SALES.XLSSheet11]Sheet11'!B3)

Here, we're instructing Excel to refer to a workbook called 96_SALES.XLS in the MY DOCUMENTS folder. This workbook isn't currently open. Notice that:

- the full workbook/worksheet address is enclosed in single quotes

- the workbook title is surrounded by square brackets

- the worksheet is also specified within the address.

Use the syntax in the examples given here in your own linking formulas.

Study the formula for B3 below:

=SUM([97_SALES.XLS]Sheet12!B3)

Here, we don't need to specify the workbook address (i.e. the drive and folder) because it is already open. Apart from this, however, the same syntax applies.

And the formula for B4:

=Sheet2!B4

This formula refers to a specific worksheet and cell within the current workbook – 98_SALES.XLS – using the standard techniques we've discussed in earlier chapters.

3D references

In the example discussed on pages 100 and 101, all the worksheets have exactly the same format in that each quarterly amount lies in the same cell on each sheet. When this is the case, you can use an alternative method of summarising the sales figures on the third sheet: 3D referencing. Using 3D references is often quicker and more convenient.

3D references consist of both of the following:

• a sheet range (i.e. the beginning and end sheets are specified, separated by a colon)

• a standard cell range

 Not all Excel functions support 3D referencing. Those that do include:

Average

Count

Max

Min

Sum

Entering a 3D reference

Select the relevant cell. Type in the required formula. As you do so, follow these rules:

1. Type =

2. Type in the appropriate function (see the Beware tip), then (

3. Type in the reference to the first worksheet, followed by a colon

4. Type in the reference to the final worksheet

5. Type !

6. Type in the cell range in the normal way, then)

7. Press Enter

In our specific example (and given that the 1997 totals are on Sheet11 and the 1998 totals on Sheet12), the formula will be:

=Sum(Sheet11:Sheet12!B3)

Hiding data (1)

If a worksheet contains a mass of information, you can temporarily hide some of the data to get a clearer overview.

Hiding rows and columns

Select the row(s) or column(s) to be hidden. Pull down the Format menu and carry out steps 1 and 2 OR 3 and 4 below, as appropriate:

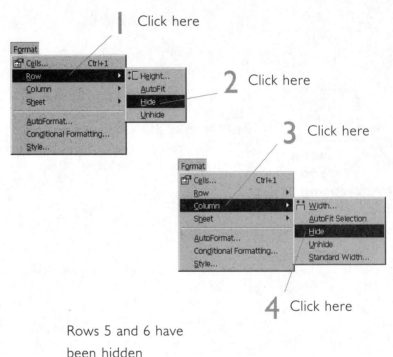

Click here

2 Click here

3 Click here

4 Click here

To unhide data, make a selection which includes the row(s) or column(s). (For instance, to unhide rows 5 and 6 in the example on the right, select rows 4-7 inclusive). Pull down the Format menu and click Row, Unhide or Column, Unhide.

Rows 5 and 6 have been hidden

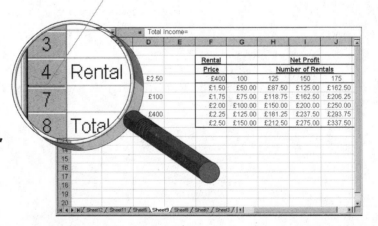

Hiding data (2)

An alternative way to hide rows or columns temporarily is to use outlining. When you apply outlining to specific row(s) or column(s) within a worksheet, Excel inserts an Outline Level Bar against the specified data. You can then specify whether the data displays or not.

Applying outlining (1)

Select one or more rows or columns. Pull down the Data menu and do the following:

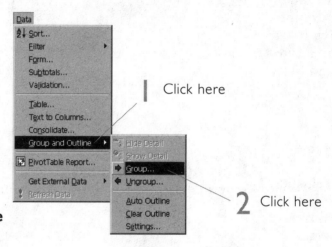

Click here

2 Click here

The Outline Level Bar – rows 5 and 6 will be hidden (see page 106)

HANDY TIP **To hide the Outline Level bar, pull down the Tools menu and click Options; activate the View tab and deselect Outline Symbols.**

Hiding data (3)

Hiding outlined data

To hide data which you've outlined, do the following:

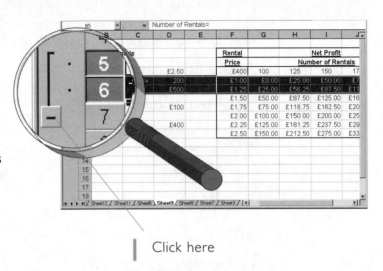

Click here

You can also hide or unhide data levels by referring to the row or column level symbols:

below the Name box.

As a general rule, click the higher number(s) to hide data, the lower numbers to reveal it.

Unhiding outlined data

To unhide data which you've outlined, do the following:

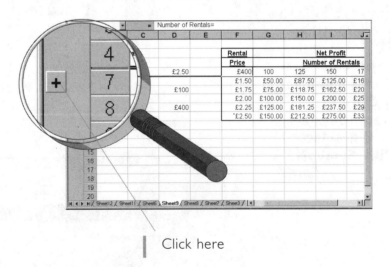

Click here

Hiding data (4)

Removing outlines

If you want to remove an outline, make a selection which includes the appropriate row(s) or column(s). In the illustration below, rows 5 and 6 have previously been outlined and are currently hidden; to remove the outlining, rows 4-7 have been selected:

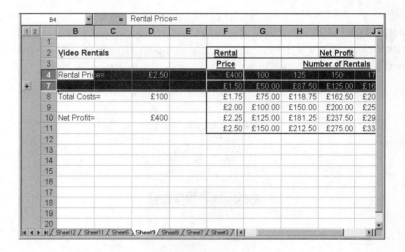

Now pull down the Data menu and do the following:

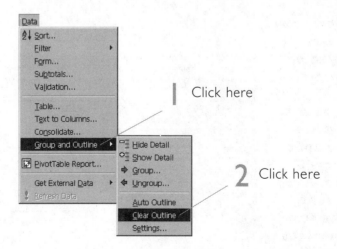

Splitting/freezing worksheets (1)

Excel has two further techniques you can use to make complex worksheets easier to understand. You can:

- split worksheets horizontally or vertically into panes

- freeze individual panes, so that the data they contain doesn't scroll

HANDY TIP

Create the precise effect you need by using split and freeze combinations.

Splitting worksheets

Select the row or column before which you want the worksheet to be split. Pull down the Window menu and do the following:

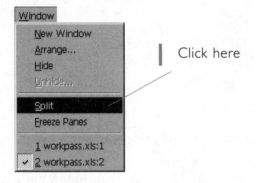

Window
New Window
Arrange...
Hide
Unhide...
Split
Freeze Panes
1 workpass.xls:1
✓ 2 workpass.xls:2

Click here

REMEMBER

Here, row 6 was selected before step 1 was performed; as a result, Excel has inserted the Split Bar below row 5.

As this is a horizontal split, dragging the scroll boxes on the right of the screen moves the respective pane up or down.

The Split Bar   Two panes

	B	C	D	E	F	G	H	I	J
1									
2	Video Rentals				Rental			Net Profit	
3					Price		Number of Rentals		
4	Rental Price=		£2.50		£400	100	125	150	175
5	Number of Rentals=		200		£1.00	£0.00	£25.00	£50.00	£75.00
6	Total Income=		£500		£1.25	£25.00	£56.25	£87.50	£118.75
7					£1.50	£50.00	£87.50	£125.00	£162.50
8	Total Costs=		£100		£1.75	£75.00	£118.75	£162.50	£206.25
9					£2.00	£100.00	£150.00	£200.00	£250.00
10	Net Profit=		£400		£2.25	£125.00	£181.25	£237.50	£293.75
11					£2.50	£150.00	£212.50	£275.00	£337.50
12									
13									
14									
15									
16									
17									
18									

B7 =

Sheet12 / Sheet11 / Sheet6 \ Sheet9 / Sheet8 / Sheet7 / Sheet3 /

Splitting/freezing worksheets (2)

Freezing panes

Do one of the following, as appropriate:

1. To freeze the top pane, select the row above which you want the split inserted.

2. To freeze the left pane, select the column to the left of which you want the split inserted.

Now pull down the Window menu and do the following:

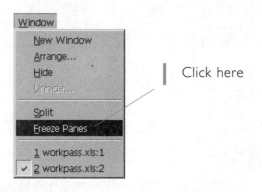

Click here

The Freeze split

HANDY TIP

Here, column E was selected before the worksheet was frozen.

This is a vertical freeze; dragging this scroll bar moves the right-hand pane to the left or right.

Splitting/freezing worksheets (3)

Redefining a split

You can adjust a split with the use of the mouse. Carry out the following:

Drag the Split Bar to a new location

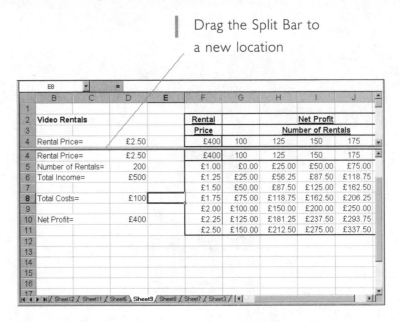

Removing a split

To remove a split, simply double-click the Split Bar.

Unfreezing a worksheet

Pull down the Window menu and do the following:

Click here

Formatting worksheets

In this chapter, you'll learn to customise cell formatting. You'll specify how cell contents align, apply fonts and type sizes and border/fill cells. You'll also format data automatically, and transfer formats between cells. Then you'll use conditional formatting to have Excel flag cells which meet specific criteria. Finally, you'll carry out data searches and use styles to make formatting even easier.

Chapter Eleven

Covers

Cell alignment (1)

By default, Excel aligns text to the left of cells, and numbers to the right. However, if you want you can change this.

You can specify alignment under two broad headings: Horizontal and Vertical.

Horizontal alignment
The main options are:

General	the default (see above)
Left	contents are aligned to the left
Center	contents are centred
Right	contents are aligned to the right
Fill	contents are duplicated so that they fill the cell
Justify	a combination of Left and Right.

Vertical alignment
Available options are:

Top	cell contents align with the top of the cell(s)
Center	contents are centred
Bottom	contents align with the cell bottom
Justify	contents are aligned along the top and bottom of the cell(s)

Most of these settings parallel features found in Word (and many other word-processors). The difference, however, lies in the fact that Excel has to align data within the bounds of cells rather than a page. When it aligns text, it often needs to employ its own version of text wrap. See 'Cell alignment (2)' for more information on this.

REMEMBER

One further horizontal option – Center across selection – centres cell contents across more than one cell (if you selected a cell range before initiating it).

HANDY TIP

You can also rotate text within cells – see 'Cell alignment (2)' for more information.

Cell alignment (2)

Other alignment features you can set are rotation and text wrap.

Rotation controls the direction of text flow within cells; you achieve this by specifying a plus (anticlockwise) or minus (clockwise) angle.

When the Wrap Text option is selected, Excel – instead of overflowing any surplus text into adjacent cells to the right – forces it onto separate lines within the host cell.

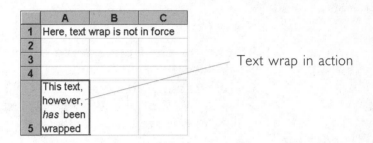

Text wrap in action

Customising cell alignment

Select the cell(s) whose contents you want to realign. Pull down the Format menu and click Cells. Carry out step 1 below. Now follow any or all of steps 2-4, as appropriate. Finally, carry out step 5.

1 Ensure the Alignment tab is active

Click here to wrap text within the holding cell(s):

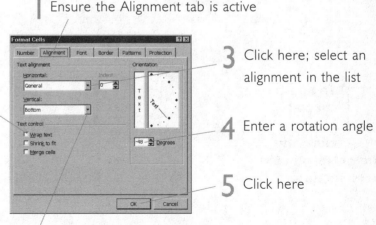

3 Click here; select an alignment in the list

4 Enter a rotation angle

5 Click here

2 Click here; select an alignment in the list

Changing fonts and attributes

Don't confuse font styles with overall styles (collections of formatting aspects). See pages 122-126 for how to use overall styles.

Excel lets you carry out the following actions on cell contents (numbers and/or text):

- apply a new font and/or type size

- apply a font style (for most fonts, you can choose from: Regular, Italic, Bold or Bold Italic)

- apply a colour

- apply a special effect (underlining, ~~strikethrough~~, superscript or subscript)

Amending the appearance of cell contents

Select the cell(s) whose contents you want to reformat. Pull down the Format menu and click Cells. Carry out step 1 below. Now follow any of steps 2-5, as appropriate, or either or both of the two tips. Finally, carry out step 6.

To underline the specified contents, click the arrow to the right of the Underline box; select an underline type in the list.

1 Ensure the Font tab is active

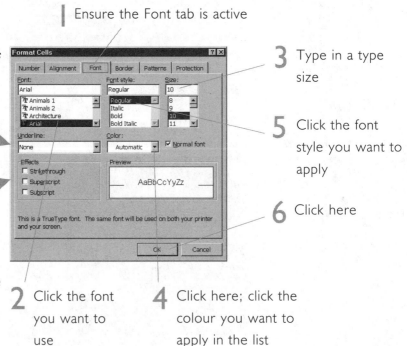

3 Type in a type size

5 Click the font style you want to apply

6 Click here

To apply a special effect, click any of the options in the Effects section.

2 Click the font you want to use

4 Click here; click the colour you want to apply in the list

Bordering cells

Excel lets you define a border around:

- the perimeter of a selected cell range

- specific sides within a cell range

You can customise the border by choosing from a selection of pre-defined border styles. You can also colour the border, if required.

Applying a cell border

First, select the cell range you want to border. Pull down the Format menu and click Cells. Now carry out steps 1 and 2 below. Step 3 is optional. Follow steps 4 and 5, as appropriate (if you're setting *multiple* border options, repeat steps 2-5 as required). Finally, carry out step 6:

1 Ensure the Border tab is active

4 Click the relevant border style option

2 Click a preset line style

3 Click here; click the colour you want to apply in the list

6 Click here

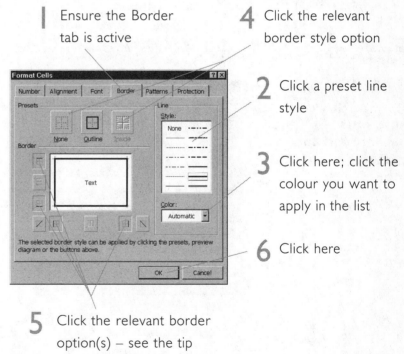

HANDY TIP

Re step 5 – clicking any of the indicated buttons borders just one side.

5 Click the relevant border option(s) – see the tip

Shading cells

Excel lets you apply the following to cells:

- a pattern

- a pattern colour

- a background colour

You can do any of these singly, or in combination. Interesting effects can be achieved by using pattern colours with coloured backgrounds.

Applying a pattern or background

First, select the cell range you want to shade. Pull down the Format menu and click Cells. Now carry out step 1. Perform step 2 to apply a *background* colour, and/or 3-4 to apply a *foreground* pattern or pattern/colour combination. Finally, follow step 5.

The Sample field previews how your background and pattern/colour will look.

| Ensure the Patterns tab is active

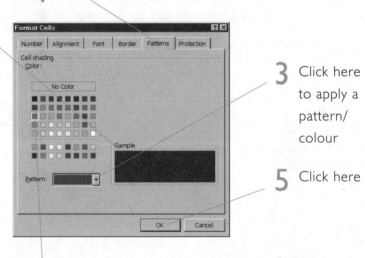

3 Click here to apply a pattern/ colour

5 Click here

2 Click a colour here to apply it as a background

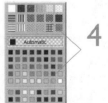

4 Click a pattern or colour

AutoFormat

Excel provides a shortcut to the formatting of worksheet data: AutoFormat.

AutoFormat consists of 16 pre-defined formatting schemes. These incorporate specific excerpts from the font, number, alignment, border and shading options discussed earlier. You can apply any of these schemes (and their associated formatting) to selected cell ranges with just a few mouse clicks. You can even specify which scheme elements you *don't* wish to use.

AutoFormat works with most arrangements of worksheet data.

Using AutoFormat

First, select the cell range you want to apply an automatic format to. Pull down the Format menu and click AutoFormat. Now carry out step 1 below. Steps 2 and 3 are optional. Finally, follow step 4.

HANDY TIP

The Sample field previews how your data will look with the specified AutoFormat.

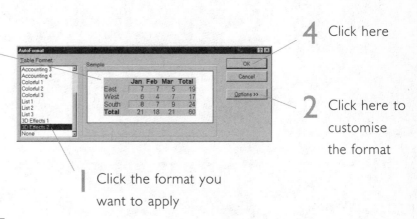

4 Click here

2 Click here to customise the format

Click the format you want to apply

REMEMBER

Re step 3 – the dialog shown here is an addition to the AutoFormat dialog.

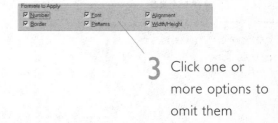

3 Click one or more options to omit them

The Format Painter

Excel provides a very useful tool which can save you a lot of time and effort: the Format Painter. You can use the Format Painter to copy the formatting attributes from cells you've previously formatted to other cells, in one operation.

Using the Format Painter

First, apply the necessary formatting, if you haven't already done so. Then select the formatted cells. Now refer to the Standard toolbar and do the following:

Re step 1 – double-click the Format Painter icon if you want to apply the selected formatting more than once. Then repeat step 2 as often as necessary.

Click here

Carry out step 2 below:

Pre-formatted text

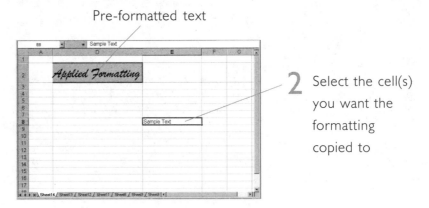

2 Select the cell(s) you want the formatting copied to

When you've finished using the Format Painter, press Esc.

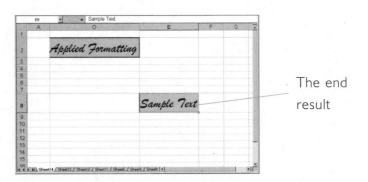

The end result

Conditional formatting

Formatting which alters cell size (e.g. font changes) can't be used as a conditional format.

You can have Excel apply conditional formats to specific cells. Conditional formats are formatting attributes (for instance, colour or shading) which Excel imposes on cells when the criteria you set are met. Conditional formats help you identify cells and monitor worksheets.

For instance, in a worksheet in which B10 is the total of the number of videos rented out, you could tell Excel to colour B10 in red if the value it contains falls below a certain level, or in blue if it exceeds it...

Applying conditional formatting

Select the relevant cell(s). Pull down the Format menu and click Conditional Formatting. Now do the following:

If you want, you can use a TRUE/ FALSE formula to define the match. Click here: Select Formula Is. Now type in the formula in the field to the right. Finally, carry out steps 3-7, as appropriate.

1 Click here; select a comparison phrase

2 Type in a match value

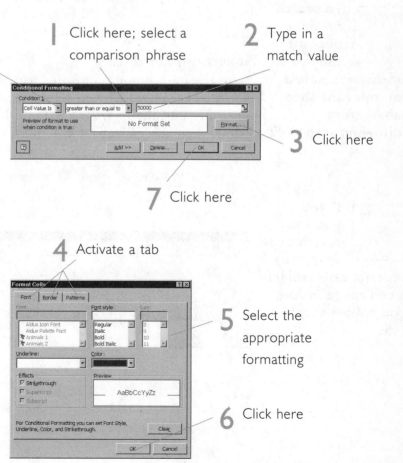

3 Click here

7 Click here

Re step 2 – complete more than one field, if necessary (in line with the comparison phrase chosen).

4 Activate a tab

5 Select the appropriate formatting

Re step 5 – the available options depend on the tab selected in step 4.

6 Click here

Find operations

Excel lets you search for and jump to text or numbers (in short, any information) in your worksheets. This is a particularly useful feature when worksheets become large and complex.

You can organise your search by rows or by columns. You can also specify whether Excel looks in:

- cells that contain formulas

- cells that don't contain formulas

Additionally, you can insist that Excel only flag *exact* matches (e.g. if you searched for '11', Excel would not find '1111'), and you can also limit text searches to text which has the case you specified (e.g. searching for 'PRODUCT LIST' would not find 'Product List').

Searching for data

Place the mouse pointer at the location in the active worksheet from which you want the search to begin. Pull down the Edit menu and click Find. Now carry out step 1 below, then any of steps 2-5. Finally, carry out step 6.

To search for data over more than one worksheet, select the relevant sheet tabs before following steps 1-6.

If you want to restrict the search to specific cells, select a cell range *before* you follow steps 1-6.

1 Type in the data you want to find

4 Click here for a case-specific search

6 Click here

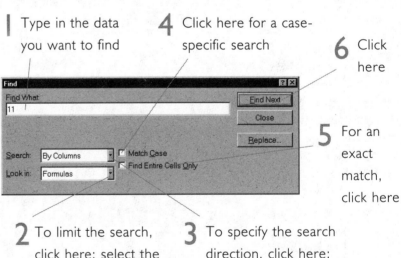

5 For an exact match, click here

2 To limit the search, click here; select the relevant option from the list

3 To specify the search direction, click here; select the relevant option from the list

Find-and-replace operations

When you search for data, you can also – if you want – have Excel replace it with something else.

Find-and-replace operations can be organised by rows or by columns. However, unlike straight searches, you can't specify whether Excel looks in cells that contain formulas or those that don't. As with straight searches, you can, however, limit find-and-replace operations to exact matches and also (in the case of text) to precise case matches.

Normally, find-and-replace operations only affect the worksheet in which they're conducted. If you want to carry out an operation over multiple worksheets, see the tip.

Running a find-and-replace operation

Place the mouse pointer at the location in the active worksheet from which you want the search to begin (or select a cell range if you want to restrict the find-and-replace operation to this). Pull down the Edit menu and click Replace. Now carry out step 1 below, then any of steps 2-5. Finally, carry out step 6, and steps 7 and/or 8 as required.

HANDY TIP

To search for and replace data over more than one worksheet, select the relevant sheet tabs before following steps 1-8.

1 Type in the data you want to find

4 Click here for a case-specific search

6 Click here to find the first occurrence

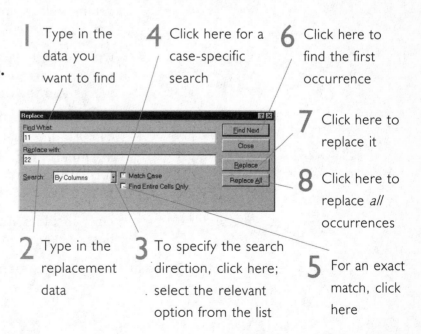

7 Click here to replace it

8 Click here to replace *all* occurrences

2 Type in the replacement data

3 To specify the search direction, click here; select the relevant option from the list

5 For an exact match, click here

Styles – an overview

Styles are named collections of associated formatting commands.

The advantage of using styles is that you can apply more than one formatting enhancement to selected cells in one go. Once a style is in place, you can change one or more elements of it and have Excel apply the amendments automatically throughout the whole of the active workbook.

Generally, new workbooks you create in Excel have the following pre-defined styles as a minimum:

Comma	Only includes numeric formatting – numerals are shown with two decimal places
Comma (0)	Only includes numeric formatting – numerals are shown with 0 decimal places
Currency	Only includes numeric formatting – numerals are shown with two decimal places and the default currency symbol
Currency (0)	Only includes numeric formatting – numerals are shown with 0 decimal places and the default currency symbol
Normal	The default. Includes numeric, alignment, font and border/shading formatting – numerals are shown with 0 decimal places
Percent	Only includes numeric formatting – data is expressed as a percentage

You can easily create (and apply) your own styles.

Creating a style

BEWARE

Keep styles simple. Select only single cells or cells which have identical formatting. Styles are not suitable for ranges of cells with different outline borders.

The easiest way to create a style is to:

1. apply the appropriate formatting enhancements to one or more specific cells and then select them

2. tell Excel to create a new style based on this formatting

First, carry out step 1 above. Then pull down the Format menu and do the following:

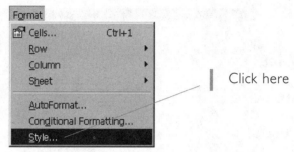

Click here

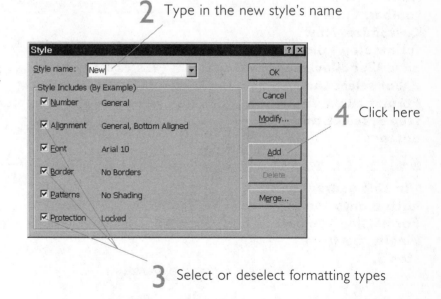

2 Type in the new style's name

HANDY TIP

Click OK when you've finished using the Style dialog.

4 Click here

3 Select or deselect formatting types

See page 124 for how to use your new style.

Applying styles

BEWARE

If you apply a style to previously formatted cells, it will override the original formatting.

Excel makes applying styles easy.

First, select the cell(s) you want to apply the style to. Pull down the Format menu and click Style. Now do the following:

Click here; in the list, click the style you want to apply

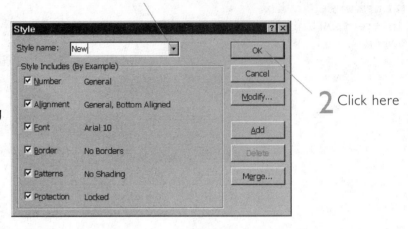

2 Click here

HANDY TIP

By default, the Formatting toolbar doesn't display the Style box.
To make it visible, right-click the toolbar. Click Customize. Now follow step 1 on page 12. Follow step 2, but select the Format menu. In step 3, select this button:

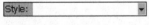

In step 4, drag the button onto the Formatting toolbar. Finally, perform step 5.

Shortcut for applying styles

Excel makes it even easier to apply styles if you currently have the Formatting toolbar on-screen. (If you haven't, pull down the View menu and click Toolbars, Formatting.)

Select the cell(s) you want to apply the style to. Then do the following:

Style box   Click here

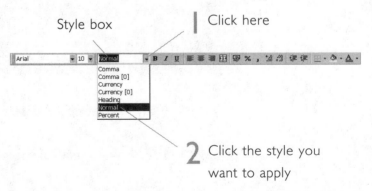

2 Click the style you want to apply

Amending styles

The easiest way to modify an existing style is to:

1. apply the appropriate formatting enhancements to one or more cells and then select them

2. use the Style dialog to select a style and tell Excel to assign the selected formatting to it

First, carry out step 1 above. Then pull down the Format menu and do the following:

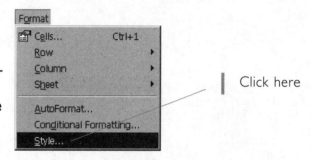

Click here

Re step 2 – you must type in the name of the style you want to amend.

Don't click the ▾ button to the right of the Style name field and select the style from the list.

2 Type in the name of the style you want to amend

Click OK when you've finished using the Style dialog.

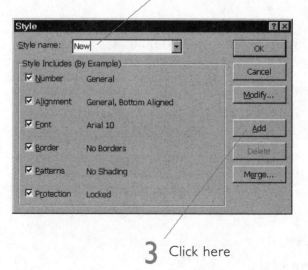

3 Click here

Deleting and copying styles

If the workbook you're copying from has styles with the same name as the target workbook, those in the target are overwritten (unless you halt the merge operation).

Good housekeeping sometimes makes it necessary to remove unwanted styles from the active document. Excel lets you do this very easily.

Another useful feature is the ability to copy ('merge') styles from one workbook to another.

Deleting styles

Pull down the Format menu and click Style. Now carry out the following steps:

Click here; in the list, click the
style you want to delete

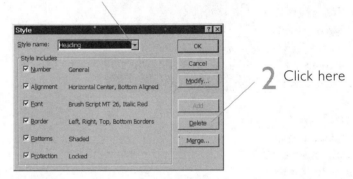

2 Click here

HANDY TIP

After step 1, below right, Excel launches the Merge Styles dialog. Do the following:

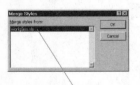

Double-click the
workbook which
contains the styles
you want to copy

Excel now imports the styles.

Copying styles

Open the workbook from which you want to copy styles, then the workbook you want to copy them into. Pull down the Format menu and click Styles. Now do the following:

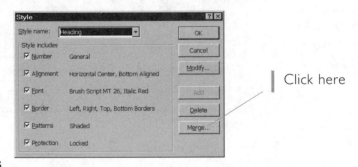

Click here

Printing worksheets

In this chapter, you'll learn how to prepare your worksheets for printing. This involves specifying the paper size and orientation, margins and page numbering, and also defining headers/footers. Then you'll launch and use Print Preview mode, to proof your worksheets. Finally, you'll specify which worksheet components should be printed, and how.

Chapter Twelve

Covers

Page setup – an overview

Excel has a special view mode: – Page Break Preview – which you can also use to ensure your worksheet prints correctly. Pull down the View menu and click Page Break Preview. Do the following (the white area denotes cells which will print, the grey those which won't):

Drag page break margins to customise the printable area

REMEMBER

Charts in separate chart sheets have unique page setup options – see Chapter 13.

Making sure your worksheets print with the correct page setup can be a complex issue, for the simple reason that most worksheets become very extensive with the passage of time (so large, in fact, that in the normal course of things they won't fit onto a single page).

Page setup features you can customise include:

- the paper size and orientation
- scaling
- the starting page number
- the print quality
- margins
- header/footer information
- page order
- which worksheet components print

Margin settings you can amend are:

- top
- bottom
- left
- right

Additionally, you can set the distance between the top page edge and the top of the header, and the distance between the bottom page edge and the bottom edge of the footer.

When you save your active workbook, all Page Setup settings are saved with it.

Setting worksheet options

The Page Setup dialog for charts in chart sheets has a special tab – see page 142 for how to use this.

Excel lets you:

- define a printable area on-screen

- define a column or row title which will print on every page

- specify which worksheet components should print

- print with minimal formatting

- determine the print direction

If you want to print a specific cell range (area), type in the address here:

Using the Sheet tab in the Page Setup dialog

Pull down the File menu and click Page Setup. Now carry out step 1 below, followed by steps 2-4 (and the tips) as appropriate. Finally, carry out step 5.

1 Ensure the Sheet tab is active

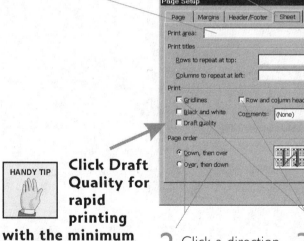

4 Type in the address of the row/column you want to use as a consistent title

5 Click here

Click Draft Quality for rapid printing with the minimum of formatting.

2 Click a direction option

3 Click a component to include or exclude it

Setting page options

Excel comes with some 17 pre-defined paper sizes which you can apply to your worksheets, in either portrait (tall) or landscape (wide) orientation. This is one approach to effective printing. Another is scaling: you can print out your worksheets as they are, or you can have Excel shrink them so that they fit a given paper size (you can even automate this process). Additionally, you can set the print resolution and starting page number.

Using the Page tab in the Page Setup dialog

Pull down the File menu and click Page Setup. Now carry out step 1 below, followed by steps 2-6 as appropriate. Finally, carry out step 7:

HANDY TIP **Re step 5 – by default, Excel numbers pages from '1'. Leave the First Page Number field setting as Auto if you want this.**

1 Ensure the Page tab is active

2 Click the orientation you need

3 Click here; click the page size you need in the drop-down list

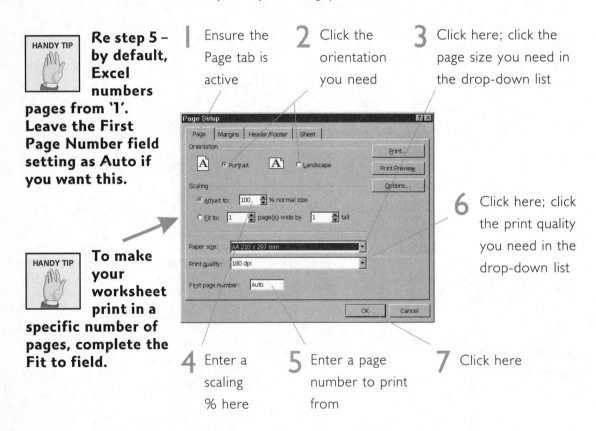

HANDY TIP **To make your worksheet print in a specific number of pages, complete the Fit to field.**

6 Click here; click the print quality you need in the drop-down list

4 Enter a scaling % here

5 Enter a page number to print from

7 Click here

Setting margin options

 Excel inserts page breaks automatically. If you need to override these, click the row, column or cell where you want the new page to begin. Pull down the Insert menu and click Page Break.

Excel lets you set a variety of margin settings. The illustration below shows the main ones:

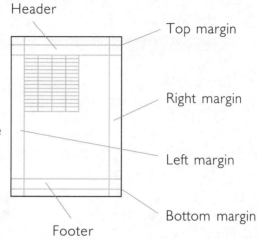

Header

Top margin

Right margin

Left margin

Bottom margin

Footer

 To view automatic page breaks, pull down the Tools menu and click Options. Activate the View tab. Ensure Page breaks is selected. Click OK.

Using the Margins tab in the Page Setup dialog

Pull down the File menu and click Page Setup. Now carry out step 1 below, followed by steps 2-3 as appropriate. Finally, carry out step 4:

1 Ensure the Margins tab is active

 To specify how your worksheet aligns on the page, click either option here:

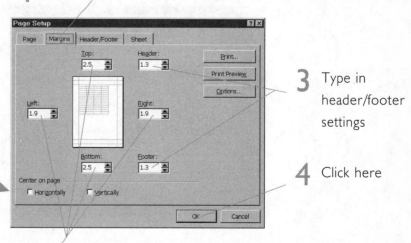

3 Type in header/footer settings

4 Click here

2 Type in the margin settings you need

Setting header/footer options

Excel provides a list of built-in header and footer settings. You can apply any of these to the active worksheet. These settings include:

- the worksheet title

- the workbook title

- the date

- the user's name

- 'confidential'

- permutations of these

Using the Header/Footer tab in the Page Setup dialog

Pull down the File menu and click Page Setup. Now carry out step 1 below, followed by steps 2-3 as appropriate. Finally, carry out step 4:

1 Ensure the Header/ Footer tab is active

2 Click here; select a header from the list

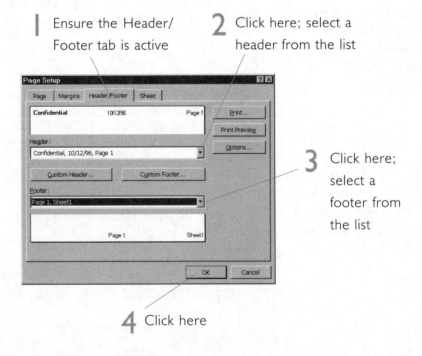

3 Click here; select a footer from the list

4 Click here

Launching Print Preview

Excel provides a special view mode called Print Preview. This displays the active worksheet exactly as it will look when printed. Use Print Preview as a final check just before you begin printing.

You can perform the following actions from within Print Preview:

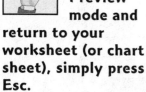

Excel's Print Preview mode has only two Zoom settings: Full Page and High-Magnification.

- moving from page to page

- zooming in or out on the active page

- adjusting most Page Setup settings

- adjusting margins visually

Launching Print Preview

Pull down the File menu and click Print Preview. This is the result:

To leave Print Preview mode and return to your worksheet (or chart sheet), simply press Esc.

Special Print Preview toolbar

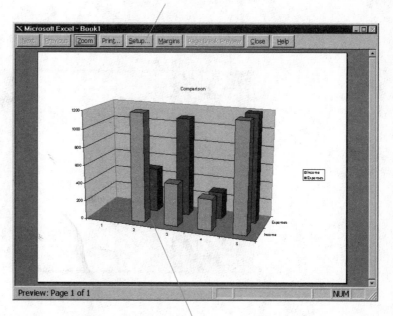

A preview of a chart sheet

See Chapter 13 for how to work with charts.

Working with Print Preview

All of the operations you can perform in Print Preview mode can be accessed via the dedicated toolbar.

REMEMBER

Click the Page Break Preview button to launch Page Break Preview – see the Handy Tip on page 128 for how to use it.

Using the Print Preview toolbar

Do any of the following, as appropriate:

1 Click here to jump to the next page

3 Click here to zoom in or out

6 Click here to launch the Page Setup dialog

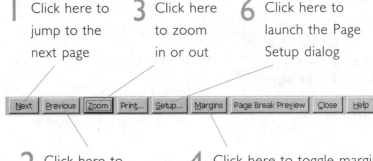

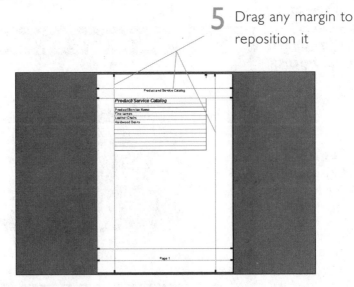

HANDY TIP

Re step 6 – see earlier topics (pages 128-132) for how to use the Page Setup dialog.

2 Click here to jump to the previous page

4 Click here to toggle margin markers on or off – then follow step 5

5 Drag any margin to reposition it

Printing worksheet data

Excel lets you specify:

• the number of copies you want printed

• whether you want the copies 'collated'. This is the process whereby Excel prints one full copy at a time. For instance, if you're printing three copies of a 10-page worksheet, Excel prints pages 1-10 of the first copy, followed by pages 1-10 of the second and pages 1-10 of the third.

• which pages (or page ranges) you want printed

• whether you want the print run restricted to cells you selected before initiating printing

You can 'mix and match' these, as appropriate.

Starting a print run

Open the workbook that contains the data you want to print. If you want to print an entire worksheet, click the relevant tab in the worksheet tab area. If you need to print a specific cell range within a worksheet, select it. Then pull down the File menu and click Print. Do any of steps 1-5. Then carry out step 6 to begin printing.

To select and print more than one worksheet, hold down Shift as you click on multiple tabs in the worksheet tab area.

REMEMBER

HANDY TIP

If you need to adjust your printer's internal settings before you initiate printing, click Properties. Then refer to your printer's manual.

Click here; select the printer you want from the list

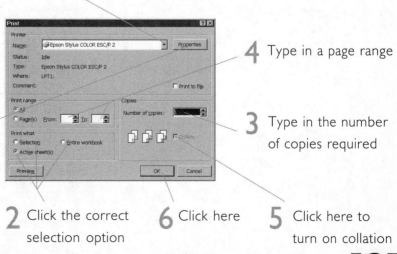

4 Type in a page range

3 Type in the number of copies required

2 Click the correct selection option

6 Click here

5 Click here to turn on collation

Printing – the fast-track approach

In earlier topics, we looked at how to customise print options to meet varying needs and worksheet sizes. However, Excel recognises that there will be times when you won't need this level of complexity. There are occasions when you'll merely want to print out your work – often for proofing purposes – with the standard print defaults applying, and with the absolute minimum of mouse actions.

The default print options are:

- Excel prints only the active worksheet

- Excel prints only 1 copy

- Excel prints all pages within the active worksheet

- collation is turned off

For this reason, Excel provides a method which bypasses the standard Print dialog, and is therefore much quicker and easier to use.

Printing with the default print options

First, click the tab that relates to the worksheet you want to print. Ensure your printer is ready. Make sure the Standard toolbar is visible. (If it isn't, pull down the View menu and click Toolbars, Standard.) Now do the following:

Click here

Excel starts printing the active worksheet immediately.

Charts and graphics

Use this chapter to learn how to create and insert new charts (both as objects within worksheets and as separate chart sheets) in order to give visual expression to your data, then save your charts to the Internet. You'll also insert – and then manipulate – pictures and clip art. Finally, you'll insert AutoShapes, extraordinarily flexible graphic shapes. All of these techniques improve worksheet impact dramatically.

Covers

Chapter Thirteen

Charting – an overview

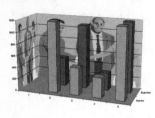

You can add a picture or clip art to chart walls. Select the wall(s) in the normal way. Then follow the procedures set out on pages 144-146.

Excel has comprehensive charting capabilities, which allow you to convert selected data into its visual equivalent. To do this, Excel offers a wide range of chart formats and sub-formats.

You can create a chart:

• as a picture within the parent worksheet

• as a separate chart sheet

Chart sheets have their own tabs in the tab area; these operate just like worksheet tabs.

Excel uses a special Wizard – the ChartWizard – to make the process of creating charts as easy and convenient as possible.

When you resize a chart, fonts rescale automatically, for increased legibility.

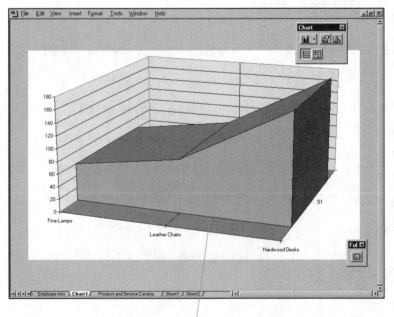

A 3-D Area chart

Creating a chart (1)

HANDY TIP **Click and hold here to have Excel preview the chart type/sub-type combination:**

First, select the cells you want converted into a chart. Pull down the Insert menu and click Chart. The first ChartWizard dialog appears. Do the following:

Click a chart type

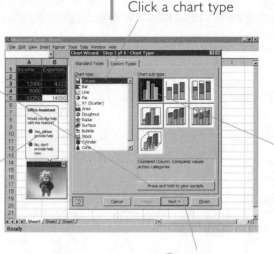

HANDY TIP **Click here if you want the Office Assistant to supply help with chart creation.**

2 Click a chart sub-type

3 Click here

HANDY TIP **Re step 4 – click the Collapse Dialog button:**

to hide the dialog temporarily while you select an alternative cell range. When you've finished, do the following:

Click here

There are three more dialogs to complete. Carry out the following steps:

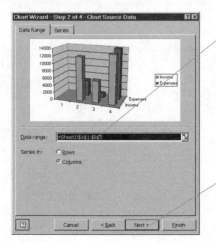

4 If you selected the wrong cells before launching the Chart Wizard, click here; then select the correct range in your worksheet

5 Click here

Creating a chart (2)

HANDY TIP

Click any of the additional tabs to set further chart options.

For example, activate the **Gridlines tab** to specify how and where gridlines display. Or click **Legend** to determine where legends (text labels) display...

Excel launches the third ChartWizard dialog. Carry out the following steps:

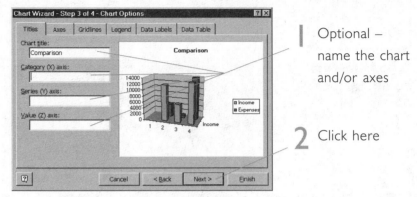

1 Optional – name the chart and/or axes

2 Click here

In the final dialog, you tell Excel whether you want the chart inserted into the current worksheet, or into a new chart sheet.

Carry out step 3 OR 4 below. Finally, perform step 5.

HANDY TIP

To convert an existing chart to a new type, select it. Pull down the Chart menu and click **Chart Type**. Now follow steps 1-3 on page 139.

Alternatively, you can apply a custom chart type. Launch the **Chart Type** dialog (as above). Activate the **Custom Types tab**. In the **Chart type** field, click a custom type. Click **OK**.

3 Click here to create a chart sheet

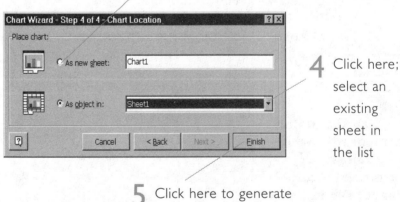

4 Click here; select an existing sheet in the list

5 Click here to generate the chart

Formatting charts

To add new data to an embedded chart, insert new rows/ columns into the worksheet. Then select the new cells. Move the mouse pointer over the selection boundary (it changes to an arrow) and drag the new data onto the chart. Excel rebuilds the chart.

To amend the formatting of a chart component, do the following:

1 Double-click the component you want to format

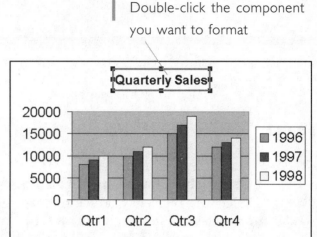

To add text to a chart, click it. Type in the text; press Enter. Excel places it in the centre of the chart; drag the text to the correct location.

2 Activate the relevant tab

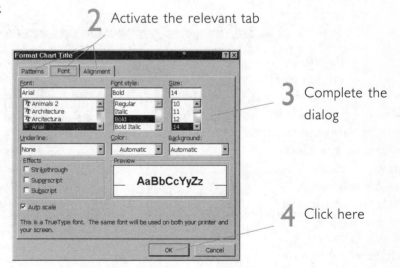

3 Complete the dialog

4 Click here

If you aren't sure what a chart component refers to, move the mouse pointer over it; Excel displays an explanatory Chart Tip:

Value Axis

Page setup for charts

Most page setup issues for charts are identical to those for worksheet data (see page 129). The main difference, however, is that the Page Setup dialog has a Chart tab (rather than a Sheet tab).

In the Chart tab, you can opt to have the chart:

- printed at full size

- scaled to fit the page

- user-defined

You can also set the print quality.

Using the Chart tab in the Page Setup dialog

Select the relevant chart. Pull down the File menu and click Page Setup. Now carry out step 1 below, followed by steps 2-3 as appropriate. Finally, carry out step 4.

REMEMBER

See Chapter 12 for detailed advice on how to print worksheets and charts.

HANDY TIP

Re step 3 – clicking Custom ensures that, when you return to the chart sheet, the chart size can be adjusted with the mouse in the normal way. The chart then prints at whatever size you set.

Ensure the Chart tab is active

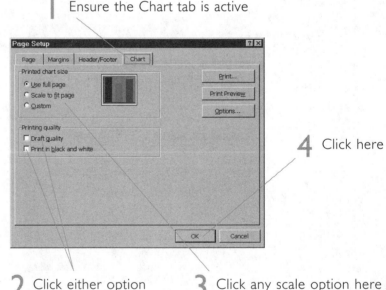

4 Click here

2 Click either option here to limit the print quality

3 Click any scale option here (see the tip)

Saving charts to the Internet

REMEMBER

Re stage ß – to publish your charts on the Web, you must have access to the Internet (e.g. via a service provider), and you must have installed a modem. For help with stage ß, consult your service provider.

For more information on the Internet in general, read a companion volume: 'Internet UK in easy steps'.

You can save Excel charts to any HTTP site on the World Wide Web. This is a two-stage process:

A.   saving your completed chart in HTML (HyperText Markup Language) format

B.   copying the HTML files to your service provider

Stage B is outside the scope of this book.

Select the chart. Pull down the File menu and click Save as HTML. Excel now launches the Internet Assistant Wizard. This consists of four dialogs. Do the following:

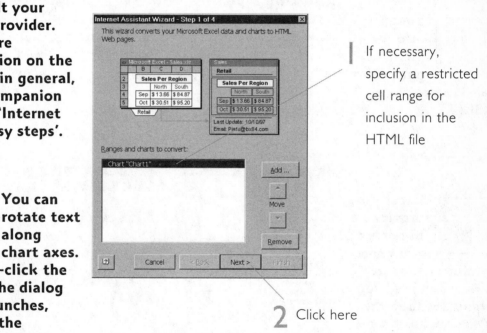

If necessary, specify a restricted cell range for inclusion in the HTML file

2 Click here

HANDY TIP

You can rotate text along chart axes.

Double-click the text. In the dialog which launches, activate the Alignment tab. Type in a plus or minus rotation in the Degrees field. Click OK.

Now complete the additional Wizard dialogs which appear (in each case, click the Next button to continue). Finally, do the following in the last dialog:

Click here

Working with pictures

Most worksheets benefit from the inclusion of colour or greyscale pictures. These can be:

- output from other programs (e.g. drawings and illustrations)

- commercial clip art

- photographs

Excel will happily translate a wide variety of third-party graphics formats.

Inserting a picture

Position the insertion point at the location in the active worksheet where you want the picture to appear. Pull down the Insert menu and click Picture, From File. Now carry out the following steps:

HANDY TIP

Once inserted into a worksheet, pictures can be resized and moved in the normal way.

HANDY TIP

You can also insert pictures onto chart walls – see page 138.

REMEMBER

Excel provides a preview of what the picture will look like when it's been imported. See the Preview box on the right of the dialog.

2 Click here. In the drop-down list, click the drive/folder which hosts the picture

4 Click here

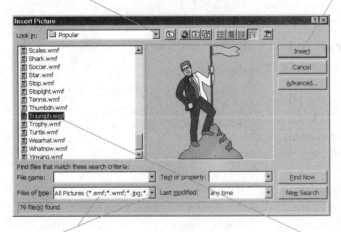

1 Make sure All Pictures is shown. If it isn't, click the arrow and select it from the drop-down list

3 Click a picture file

Inserting clip art (1)

If the Clip Gallery *isn't* currently installed on your computer, you'll need to re-run the original installation program to rectify this.

If the Office Clip Gallery is installed on your computer, you can use it to insert clip art. However, you may need to import the relevant images into the Gallery first...

Importing clip art into the Clip Gallery

Pull down the Insert menu and click Picture, Clip Art. Now carry out the following steps:

1 Click here

Re step 3 – here we're importing POPULAR.CAG, a relatively brief selection of clip art images copied to your hard disk during installation. POPULAR.CAG is located in the following folder:

msoffice\clipart\pcsfiles\

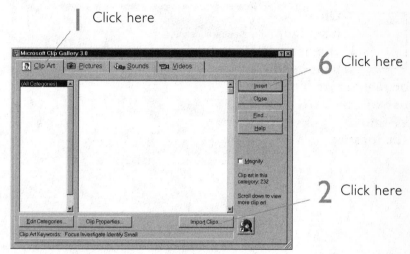

6 Click here

2 Click here

3 Click here; in the list, click the appropriate drive/ folder – see the Remember tip

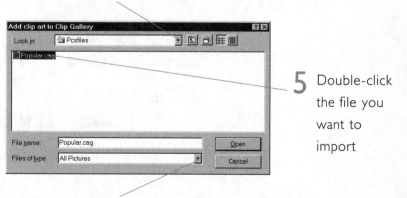

5 Double-click the file you want to import

If you installed Excel from the Office CD, you'll find additional clip art files in the CLIPART folder.

4 Click here; select All Pictures in the list

Inserting clip art (2)

Adding clip art to worksheets

Go to the worksheet into which you want the clip art added. Pull down the Insert menu and click Picture, Clip Art. Now carry out the following steps:

Activate the Clip Art tab

HANDY TIP

Once inserted, clip art can be moved or resized with the use of standard Windows techniques.

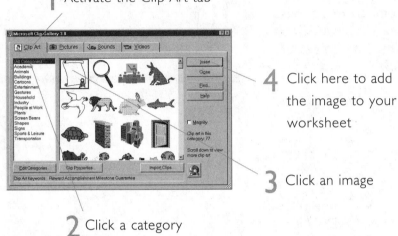

4 Click here to add the image to your worksheet

3 Click an image

2 Click a category

A blank worksheet with an added clip art image:

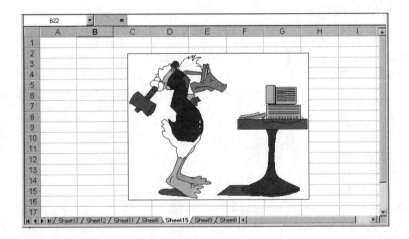

Using AutoShapes (1)

To add text to an inserted AutoShape, right-click it. In the menu, click Add Text. The insertion point appears in the centre; type in the text. Click outside the AutoShape.

AutoShapes represent an extraordinarily flexible and easy-to-use way to insert a wide variety of shapes into your worksheets. Once inserted, they can be:

- resized

- rotated/flipped

You can also add text to AutoShapes – see the Handy Tips. Excel automatically aligns text optimally.

Text which has been inserted into an AutoShape becomes an integral part of it: any changes you make to the AutoShape also affect the text.

Inserting an AutoShape

Refer to the Drawing toolbar – if it isn't currently visible, pull down the View menu and click Toolbars, Drawing. Do the following:

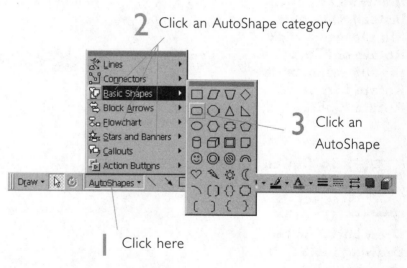

2 Click an AutoShape category

3 Click an AutoShape

Click here

You can use a shortcut to insert AutoShapes. Follow step 1. Then simply click where you want the AutoShape inserted. Now resize it appropriately – see page 148.

Now carry out these steps:

1. Place the mouse pointer where you want your AutoShape to start.

2. Hold down the left mouse button.

3. Drag out the shape.

4. Release the mouse button when you've finished.

Using AutoShapes (2)

Resizing AutoShapes

Select the AutoShape. Now do the following:

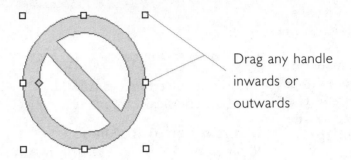

Drag any handle
inwards or
outwards

 To rotate in 90° stages, don't follow steps 1 or 2. Instead, click here: **In the menu, click Rotate or Flip. In the sub-menu, click Rotate Left or Rotate Right.**

Rotating AutoShapes

Select the AutoShape. Now refer to the Drawing toolbar and do the following:

Click here

 To 'flip' an AutoShape, select it. Click the Draw button in the Drawing toolbar. In the menu, click Rotate or Flip, followed by Flip Horizontal or Flip Vertical.

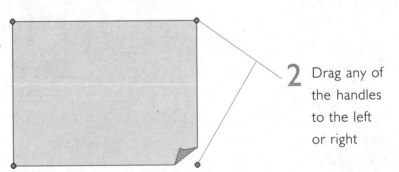

2 Drag any of
the handles
to the left
or right

Macros/customisation

This chapter shows you how to automate frequently performed tasks by recording them as macros and playing them back whenever necessary. You'll also learn to associate the macros you create with toolbar buttons, keystrokes and menu entries, to make it even easier and more convenient to use macros. Finally, you'll discover how to create new toolbars.

Covers

Chapter Fourteen

Recording a macro (1)

Excel lets you automate any task which you undertake frequently. You do this by recording it as a macro. A macro is a recorded series of commands which can be 'rerun' at will. Using macros can save you a considerable amount of time and effort.

Once recorded, macros can be rerun:

- with the use of a special dialog

- by clicking a toolbar button

- by pressing a keystroke combination (defined when you record the macro)

- by clicking a special menu entry

Recording a macro

First, plan out (preferably on paper) the precise sequence of actions involved in the task you want to record. Pull down the Tools menu and do the following:

Here, we're recording a macro which will embolden and italicise cell contents in one operation (actions which can be implemented separately by pressing Ctrl+ß and Ctrl+I respectively).
  This is a very simple example, for the sake of clarity; however, you can easily record complex procedures as macros.

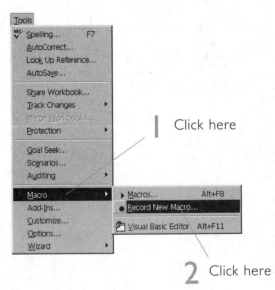

Recording a macro (2)

HANDY TIP

Re step 2 – Excel assumes you want the shortcut key which will launch the macro to be Ctrl+? (where ? is any letter).

However, you can also incorporate Shift into any keystroke combination; simply hold down one Shift key as you type in the letter. For example, to have the macro invoked by pressing Ctrl+Shift+H, hold down Shift and type in H.

Now carry out the following steps:

Name the macro

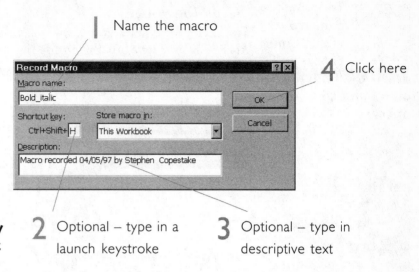

4 Click here

2 Optional – type in a launch keystroke

3 Optional – type in descriptive text

Perform the actions you want to record. When you've finished, do the following:

The Stop Recording toolbar

5 Click here

Running a macro

You can run macros in a variety of ways.

HANDY TIP

To launch a macro via a menu entry, pull down the relevant menu and click the entry:

The dialog route

First, select the cells you want to apply the macro to. Press Alt+F8. Now carry out the following steps:

Our macro as a new entry – see page 153

Click a macro

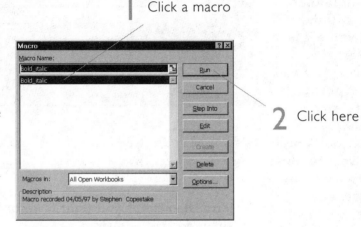

2 Click here

REMEMBER

By default, macro toolbar buttons look like this:

The toolbar route

If you've created a special toolbar button and allocated the macro to it (see page 153 for how to do this), select the relevant cell(s) and do the following:

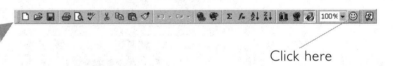

Click here

REMEMBER

Here, the macro button has been added to the Standard toolbar.

The keystroke route

If you've allocated a keystroke combination to the macro during the creation process (see page 151 for how to do this), select the cell(s) and press the relevant keys.

For example, and to continue the original example from pages 150-151, to italicise and embolden cell contents in one operation, press:

Ctrl+Shift+H

Assigning macros to toolbars

To assign a macro to a new toolbar button, first make sure the toolbar is visible (see page 11 for how to do this). Move the mouse pointer over the toolbar and right-click once. In the menu which appears, click Customize. Now do the following:

HANDY TIP

You can add macros as menu entries.
Follow steps 1 & 2. In step 3, drag this button:

`   Custom Menu Item   `

onto the menu of your choice. Now right-click the resultant menu entry. In the menu which launches, click in the Name field. Replace the default name with a new one (but leave the ampersand) – for instance:
&Bold/Italic.
Follow steps 6 & 7 to assign a macro to the new entry. Finally, carry out step 8.

| Ensure this tab is active

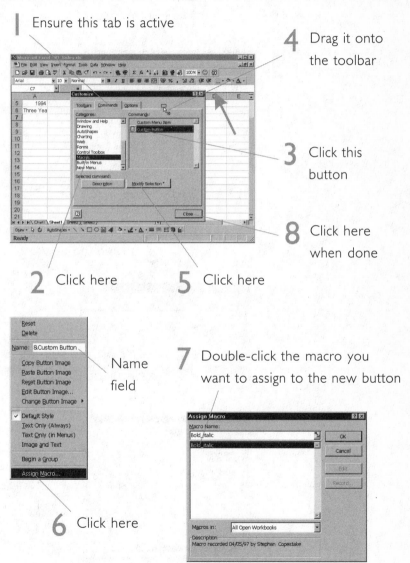

4 Drag it onto the toolbar

3 Click this button

8 Click here when done

2 Click here

5 Click here

Name field

6 Click here

7 Double-click the macro you want to assign to the new button

Creating custom toolbars

You can easily create customised toolbars.

Creating a new toolbar

Pull down the Tools menu and click Customize. Now do the following:

Activate this tab

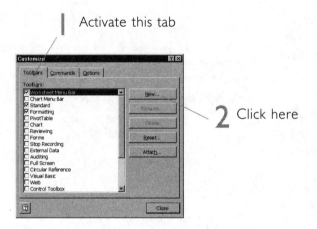

2 Click here

3 Name the new toolbar

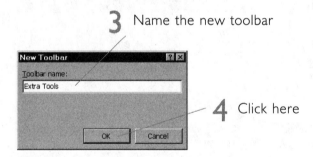

4 Click here

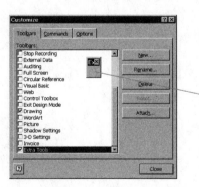

Excel creates the new toolbar, currently blank. Follow steps 1-5 on page 12 to add buttons to it

Index